The
MIRACLES
AMONG US

The
MIRACLES
AMONG US

How God's Grace Plays
a Role in Healing

Dr. Marc Siegel

Foreword by Shannon Bream

FOX
NEWS
books

THE MIRACLES AMONG US. Copyright © 2025 by Fox News
Network, LLC. Foreword copyright © 2025 by Shannon Bream.
All rights reserved. Printed in the United States of America.
No part of this book may be used or reproduced in any manner
whatsoever without written permission except in the case of brief
quotations embodied in critical articles and reviews. For information,
address HarperCollins Publishers, 195 Broadway, New York, NY
10007. In Europe, HarperCollins Publishers, Macken House,
39/40 Mayor Street Upper, Dublin 1, D01 C9W8, Ireland.

HarperCollins books may be purchased for educational, business, or sales promotional use. For information, please email the
Special Markets Department at SPsales@harpercollins.com.

hc.com

Fox News Books imprint and logo are
trademarks of Fox News Network, LLC.

FIRST EDITION

Library of Congress Cataloging-in-Publication Data has been
applied for.

ISBN 978-0-06-342628-3

25 26 27 28 29 LBC 12 11 10 9 8

To Annette and Bernard,

Two centenarians in love,

My parents.

"Honor your father and your mother,

that your days may be long upon the land which

the Lord your God is giving you."

—Exodus 20:12

CONTENTS

Foreword by Shannon Bream   xi

Introduction   xvii

PART I
PRAYERS FROM THE HEART

Chapter 1   The Most Courageous Baier   3

Chapter 2   Damar   17

Chapter 3   Breakthrough   31

Chapter 4   The Albert Schweitzer of Sudan   41

Chapter 5   The Pharmacist and the Baby   57

Chapter 6   Team 43   65

Chapter 7   The Rebbe   83

PART II
PRAYERS FOR THE SOUL

Chapter 8   The Doctor at Lourdes   99

Chapter 9   Dodie Osteen and Her World of Healing   111

Chapter 10   Still Alive in the Hungarian Forest   119

Chapter 11   Dr. Ellay Hogeg-Golan   131

CONTENTS

Chapter 12 Montgomery MD   151

Chapter 13 Dan the Man   165

Chapter 14 Congressman Scalise   187

Chapter 15 Shane   203

Chapter 16 Back from the Dead   219

Epilogue: A Prayer for My Patients   231

Acknowledgments   237

Notes   241

x

FOREWORD

by Shannon Bream

STOP WHAT YOU'RE DOING! RIGHT now, go take a look at yourself. It doesn't matter where or how and, yes, it may sound corny—but just do it. Grab the compact from your purse or check out your reflection in the toaster as you're scrambling to get breakfast and get out the door. Say to yourself, "I am a miracle!" You truly are, no ifs, ands, or buts. Every breath that you take, every time your heart beats or the synapses in your brain fire off instructions to the inter-connected systems keeping you alive, something supernatural is happening.

There is no one else in the world who will ever have the exact molecular and genetic makeup that you do—even if you've got a twin! I believe God crafts each and every life as a unique creation to be celebrated. Every day you live is a testament to phenomenal circuitry working together with precision and mystery. But sometimes (eventually, for all of us) those systems run up against human frailty—maybe it's environmental; maybe it was always going to be a part of your family lineage. In any case, you need another miracle.

I can testify to it in my own life, and the lives of others: Miracles still happen. They may not arrive in the way that we so desperately hope, but I do believe that the fervent prayers of a righteous person are powerful (James 5:16). Anyone struggling through a health challenge needs hope. Hope and faith sustain each other and make it possible to keep fighting, and that's what you'll find in these pages.

If you worry that your faith isn't strong enough, consider what happens every time you sit down at your desk or dining room table. You don't think twice about whether that chair is going to be steady enough to hold you. Experience tells you it will; it has supported you over and over again. The more time you spend resting in the belief that God knows every detail of your life, and when you take the time to look back and acknowledge the ways you've survived other seemingly insurmountable challenges, the more you begin to realize that the foundation of your faith has always been in process.

I feel deeply blessed that I grew up in a home that had faith at its core. Frankly, there were times we didn't have much else! But relying on God's faithfulness when times were hard and resources were low helped me to grow roots that blossomed into beautiful, unbreakable cords of strength when I needed them most. If you know my story, you know that there were years I lived through chronic, agonizing pain. And that's when I began praying for my own miracle.

I bounced from doctor to doctor, desperately seeking answers to the excruciating pain that had taken over my life. At the very least, I needed a diagnosis—a name—to put to the suffering I was struggling to survive one day at a time. I withdrew, I hid my desperation, and I became despondent. I spent what little energy I had putting on a happy face for the world while spiraling down into a pit of darkness. Only my precious husband, Sheldon, knew the depths of my anguish. He was the one who pulled me back from the edge when I felt I could no longer go on. You see, I'd given up on the medical establishment after being shut down by a physician who told me, "You're very emotional." I've likened it to being thrown a lead weight when I felt like I was drowning, rather than the life raft I so desperately needed.

While sitting on a bed one Sunday night, as I poured out the truth to my husband of how hopeless I'd become, we decided to pray (again). This time was a little different. Rather than pray for complete healing, which I'd done endless times, that night I prayed that if God wasn't planning to heal me, He would give me someone to help me through. The apostle Paul's story in 2 Corinthians was constantly on my mind. He'd begged God to take a "thorn" from Him, but that's not what his Heavenly Father decided to do. Instead, He reminded Paul, "My grace is sufficient for you, for my power is made perfect in weakness."

Equipped with that reminder, I decided that my miracle might look a little different than I'd initially imagined. It came in the form of a wonderful physician who not only diagnosed me but also started me on the path to managing my condition and my pain in a way that gave me my life back. I spent years in his care before he retired, and I often referred to him as my "answer to prayer" when I walked into his office. No, my miracle wasn't what I expected, but it was exactly what I needed. It deepened my faith, made me much more empathetic, and eventually brought me physical relief.

This book is full of encouraging stories that remind us miracles do come in all kinds of packages. A good friend recently shared the story of a real-life medical miracle in her own congregation. A young man fresh off a CT scan showing spots all over his liver (including one the size of an orange) decided to ask the church to get together and cover him in prayer. That was despite the guidance that he should enter the hospital for a biopsy and medical treatment right away. The prayer service his church held was unabashedly, boldly about asking for something unexplainable to happen. When he returned days later for all the follow-up scans and tests . . . the spots were gone. Every one of them, including that orange! He described the doctors as "completely confounded and confused." But he and his church family knew exactly what had happened!

Medical advancements are a blessing, and gifted doctors are servants at heart, but not everything that happens in an examination room can be explained in a textbook. Dr. Siegel is a selfless physician who is always looking to care for people in ways that improve their lives. He watches out for us! But even he will admit his expertise has limits, and he's filled this inspiring book with stories of what happens when divine intervention is the only explanation for the turnaround to a situation that seemed beyond hope. None of us is ever past that point, so enjoy these miracles and keep expecting your own—one prayer at a time.

The
MIRACLES
AMONG US

〜

INTRODUCTION

THERE ARE MEDICAL MIRACLES. I see them every day. So do you.

You may not recognize them right away. Nor do I. They are far more common than anyone knows about or admits. We tend to define them too rigidly. A miracle may not be a flash from the sky or a paralyzed person walking again or a blind man seeing, but rather an accumulation of coincidences that, taken together, are nearly impossible to predict. Sometimes the miracle lurks just below the surface. Sometimes, as Cardinal Timothy Dolan, archbishop of New York, told me in an interview, the miracle is not the one you pray for or are expecting but is simply the one God has decided to give.

A miracle may be a sign that has nothing to do with the actual medicine of the situation, but an occurrence that immediately wraps that medicine in miraculous circumstances of hope and recovery. The famed Miracle Hunter, theologian Michael O'Neill, believes that big miracles are real but smaller medical miracles are more common. He says that all religions pray for the sick in their own way. He told me in an interview that Catholics have a unique approach to evaluating miracles, investigating them thoroughly, and trying to ascertain that the miracle isn't possible by any known science. O'Neill says Catholics "care more about proving that miracles are true than any other faith. They typically want and need to validate them in order to move sainthood causes." To be canonized as a saint in Roman Catholicism, a candidate must be proven to have had "heroic virtue" while alive and to have been involved in the occurrence of two separate miracles.

Cardinal Dolan has a much less rigid definition of miracles than the Church does. Dolan departs from the orthodoxy of the Catholic Church by focusing on what he calls "soft miracles," often meaning faith combined with advances in medicine where a skilled physician serves as "the hands of God." The cardinal's niece miraculously survives a deadly cancer with a spontaneous remission, but when asked if it is due to direct divine intervention with everyone praying for her, her mother replies, "That and Dr. Berginelli" (the oncologist). This wisdom is profound. I have found that these miracles are occurring everywhere, in medical practices and in daily life. Innovations in care combined with faith are producing miracles all around the world. There are Dr. Berginellis everywhere you look.

In Judaism, we believe that medical miracles exist as a way of God working in the world. Despite Torah stories of manna falling from the sky or the sudden parting of the Red Sea, we don't focus on the need to "prove" miracles. Judaism accepts that there could be a rational explanation while at the same time a manifestation of God's beneficence. A miracle can be supernatural but doesn't have to be. Daily life itself is a miracle from God. O'Neill tells me that Protestants also believe "wholeheartedly in medical miracles and have a tradition of believing they are for real." But they don't have a rigorous investigation.

Different Protestant traditions also have varying views on what counts as a miracle, how often miracles occur, and whether they ceased happening after the Bible was completed. Though there is a debate among Protestants about what constitutes a miracle, most believe God works through human ingenuity and technology while remaining in control.

Hinduism attributes medical miracles to God or avatars of God or saints. A famous story of a Hindu miracle dating back a thousand years concerns a young man named Nambi, who filled in for his father at a temple to Ganesha. When Nambi begged, the statue of Ganesha ate the food offerings before it.

Jainism has an understanding of medical miracles that is in between the Chinese religions, which deny them, and Hinduism, which acknowledges them. Jainism believes nothing happens randomly and not everything can be explained by rational explanations. Sometimes faith is the only explanation for an event, such as when saffron water began to trickle from a stone carving in a Jain temple.

I want to tell you about one man who is 101 years old, surviving despite an artificial heart valve, a pacemaker, and several cardiac stents. He has had to overcome severe COVID, which laid him flat at the onset of the pandemic (he said he would never rise from the couch, but took hydroxychloroquine and was better the next day); a bowel obstruction due to an incarcerated hernia that leaked and poured out stool and took months to heal; weeks spent on a respirator; a broken hip; and over three years of dialysis. He is not the only patient I know of to receive dialysis or a new heart valve, or undergo major surgery with severe complications at an advanced age and survive, but he is the only one with his mental faculties completely intact. After his bowel surgery, he didn't take a single opioid, and when they asked him where he was, he made a joke by pretending he was in a field hospital in Ukraine.

This man, whose name is Bernie, is a World War II Navy vet. He worked on the moon projects in the 1960s as an engineer and helped develop the famed fail-safe CWEA system on the lunar module, a precursor of artificial intelligence that enabled the astronauts of Apollo 13 to return home safely, stuffed inside the LEM when the command module failed. His team won a national citation for this accomplishment.

Dr. Alan Zelcer, a prominent cardiologist, grew very fond of Bernie and brought him to the hospital in Delray, Florida, several times for lifesaving procedures including, finally, when the hernia was strangulating his bowel. But it was Dr. Steven Wexner, one of the top colon surgeons in the country, and his staff at Cleveland Clinic in Weston, Florida, who managed the hole in Bernie's bowel and allowed it to heal on its own without an additional surgery that would have likely killed him. Healing from this was unheard-of at this advanced age, as Bernie became the oldest person in the history of the hospital to have his respiratory failure managed via a ventilator. Dialysis followed, then weeks of rehab and a life-threatening infection from one of the indwelling catheters, until finally Bernie was brought up to New York on a commercial flight by a nurse's aide named Glen, a deeply religious man who has been living with him and his wife (age one hundred) ever since.

Now Bernie has been receiving dialysis at NYU Langone Hospital–Long Island for over three years, with the expert guidance and oversight of Dr. Naveed Masani, head of the dialysis unit. His hip was repaired under anesthesia at age ninety-nine by an amazing orthopedist, Dr. Nicole Stevens, at the same hospital.

Bernie's survival does not represent a single miracle but is an accumulation of one miracle on top of another with the unerring care of incredible doctors and nurses. This is how God often works in health care, by combinations of narrowly missed endings and barely successful treatments, by extension through tireless physicians and their teams who integrate amazing new science and technology and then go beyond it, refusing to give up hope. The accumulation of these narrow escapes from death is bound together with the glue of hope, courage, and faith. Bernie has always been a man of science, but his continued survival is an act of faith. If you ask him what keeps him going, he says it is the love for his wife, whom he doesn't want to leave alone. "I need to be here for her," he says. "I will be here for her." Their idea of romance these days is a visit to the office of Dr. Stevens, who has successfully repaired both their hips, a pin in his and a nail in hers.

As I am certain you've guessed by now, Bernie is my father, and his wife, Annette, is my mother.

I feel that God repays kindness and that goodwill toward others may be repaid by miracles as your conduit of kindness is refilled. It may be difficult to see this during times of great suffering, but it becomes clear over time. As Cardinal Dolan says, God performs the miracles he wants, not necessarily the ones you are asking him to do. But in my parents' case, God's answer to our prayers has gone well beyond our hopes.

PART I

Prayers
from the
Heart

CHAPTER 1

The Most Courageous Baier

BRET BAIER, LONGTIME HOST OF *Special Report* on the Fox News Channel, is a Pentagon correspondent for Fox in 2002 (with frequent assignments in Iraq and Afghanistan) when he meets the love of his life, Amy Hills, on a blind date. They marry two years later, and he is named Fox News' White House correspondent in 2007.

That same year, Amy Baier is pregnant with the couple's first child, a boy.

In his book *Special Heart: A Journey of Faith, Hope, Courage and Love*, Bret recounts that when Amy goes to one of her early checkups during pregnancy, a doctor conducting an ultrasound thinks he hears a slight heart echo. However, he concludes that it is just a problem with the machine. Apart from that, things are going very smoothly.

When the Baiers' baby, whom they name Paul, is born at Sibley Memorial Hospital in Washington, DC, the doctors tell the parents that their new son is completely fine. But Beth Kennedy, one of the nurses, says that he's pale. Others notice it too and think it might be from a bacterial infection. Beth calls for a cardiologist to come to check, and though the Baiers don't know it, this is the beginning of a miracle.

Not far from Sibley, Dr. Gerard Martin, who is one of the heads of pediatric cardiology at Children's National Hospital in Washington, is driving his son to a soccer game. When the hospital staff put a page out, Dr. Martin answers the page because he has a few minutes to spare, and he comes in to do Paul's echocardiogram in the neonatal/cardiac intensive care unit.

After the echocardiogram and additional tests, Dr. Martin meets with Bret and Amy and tells them, "I need to talk to you about your son." Amy has sheer terror in her eyes as he says the words that no parent wants to hear. "Your son has a complex heart disease. . . . His heart is built wrong. . . . If your son doesn't have surgery within the next two weeks, he's not going to make it."

For the Baiers, time stops. They had been told throughout Amy's pregnancy that Paul was perfect. They are shocked. How can this be happening? Dr. Martin tells them that Paul has at least five different congenital heart defects. Paul is transferred to Children's National Hospital.

Both raised as Catholics, Bret and Amy are people of faith. But now they are thinking, "Why us, Lord? Why did this have to happen to us?" Bret finds himself constantly praying to God, pleading that he will get to see his son grow up.

When I interview Bret and Amy more than seventeen years after Paul's birth, I am struck by how cohesive of a team they make. They complete each other's sentences and are always supportive of each other, driven by love and faith. In my many years of experience as a practicing internist, I have found that the mental and physical trials of taking care of a sick child wear a parent's health and either bring a couple closer together or tear them apart.

"Fear is all-consuming at the beginning," says Bret. "It gets to the point where Amy becomes the oldest patient in Children's because the stress gets to her, and she hyperventilates and collapses."

Amy is monitored and quickly recovers and eventually—day by day—the couple grows stronger, and they come up with the mantra "We're one day closer to getting Paul home." This helps them manage each day. Meanwhile, Bret asks thousands of questions and is obsessed with every beep and blip of Paul's data on a screen. Amy is obsessed with making sure Paul feels her, and she cuddles with him.

Over the years, the fear will come and go, but it is always intense whenever Bret and Amy have to watch Paul being rolled on the gurney into the operating room. "I want to be on that gurney myself," says Bret.

At Children's National, tiny Paul is hooked up to lines and machines and monitors. Bret is told by one of the nurses that Paul is having an extremely difficult time getting oxygen to flow from his lungs to his heart. Amy diverts herself from Paul's suffering by focusing on breastfeeding her tiny infant. Meanwhile, Dr. Richard Jonas, one of the top pediatric heart surgeons in the world, is assigned to Paul's case. He is out of the country but will be returning in a few days.

Paul is suffering from transposition of the great arteries,

one of the most common congenital heart lesions found in neonates in the first week of life, where there is not enough oxygen being delivered to the tissues. The aorta, which is supposed to feed the body with essential nutrients, in this case arises from the right ventricle of the heart instead of the left and pumps oxygen-poor blood to the rest of the body, where tissues are starving. At the same time, the pulmonary arteries come off the left ventricle instead of the right and bring oxygen-rich blood back to the lungs rather than to the rest of the body, where it is needed. Tissues and organs will die of oxygen deprivation unless something is done immediately. Paul's arteries are also much smaller than they should be, and both the pulmonary and the aortic valves are narrowed.

He also has two holes in his heart: one in his ventricle (the pump) and the other in the upper chambers that allow blood to flow (atrium). The vast majority of infants with these complex anatomical heart problems don't survive. Paul is placed on a prostaglandin drug to keep his vessels open as he is prepared for surgery.

In spite of the dire circumstances, Amy and Bret have faith that the hopes and dreams they have for Paul may still one day come to pass. While praying together in the small hospital chapel, Bret discovers a verse in the New Testament book of Hebrews, which has been left open to chapter 11, verse 1: "Faith is the assurance of things hoped for, the conviction of things not seen." They focus on this verse and sense that the Lord is guiding them. Bret also believes that Paulie himself has strong survival skills, that he is "a fighter with a warrior spirit."

They decide to have him baptized right there in the neonatal/cardiac intensive care unit. Slowly, Bret and Amy absorb the prayers and support of those around them and become more trusting of doctors as they receive more energy and clarity from the team.

There's another child in the hospital who has congenital heart problems. Her name is Maggie, and Bret and Amy become friendly with her parents. Only nine months old, Maggie has been in and out of Children's National throughout her short life, and has had nine surgeries already. Her parents and the Baiers pray for each other's child.

Bret and Amy are running out of time with Paul when Dr. Jonas returns to town and studies Paul's case. Luckily, Dr. Jonas has a lot of experience operating on these conditions. Now twelve days old, Paul is growing stronger, but his oxygen level is declining. He will need to be kept alive during the surgery by a heart-lung machine. There is a big question of whether there is enough room in Paul's tiny chest to use his own artery as a patch or whether Dr. Jonas will have to sew in a donated aorta from another newborn who didn't live. This aorta will then have to be replaced in a few years as the rest of the heart grows in size around it.

Dr. Jonas meets with Amy and Bret and describes his habit of studying the pictures of the heart and the scenario over and over the night before, rehearsing the operation. He won't know if there is room in the chest for Paul's own arterial patch until he is in there. Jonas assures the frantic parents that he expects Paul to make it with a "fixed and working heart. Your son will live."

The surgery goes very well, but the incredibly experienced surgeon says to Bret and Amy afterward that "this is as long and as complicated as any surgery we've done." They are unable to do the one-time fix, and must use a donated graft, which will mean repeated surgeries down the line.

The same day as Paul's surgery, Maggie dies. Her kidneys failed. And yet Maggie's mom somehow summons the strength to call Bret to ask how Paul did in surgery. This is truly humbling to Bret. "She has just lost Maggie. So the power of that . . . to pick up the phone in that grief to make sure that Paul is doing well or to send her best. You know, that's power."

Paul recovers from the surgery and goes home. Amy and Bret are overflowing with gratitude and joy that their miracle child is home and inspiring them. The doctors are astounded by the speed and success of Paul's recovery.

Unfortunately, just a few weeks later, Paul needs stomach surgery for pyloric stenosis, a separate issue (narrowing in the stomach outlet) that miraculously doesn't impede his recovery from heart surgery. Several months after that, he requires a second angioplasty (balloon) to open his pulmonary artery, which has narrowed. (A previous angioplasty had been done on the aortic arch the month before.) He is also found to have a pseudo-aneurysm (a bulging) in the pulmonary artery that will require another surgery soon.

In the meantime, Paul continues to grow stronger, and when he is ten months old, Dr. Jonas has to operate again to replace the original donated baby aorta with another one. Paul is resilient and recovers quickly.

By the time Paul is six years old and about to enter kindergarten in 2013, he has already had seven angioplasties. And now he will need a third open-heart operation so that Dr. Jonas can replace his second donated baby aorta with a newer, larger one. Paul has been having chest pains and difficulty breathing. Dr. Deneen Heath, Paul's pediatric cardiologist, is monitoring him closely.

Prior to the operation, Bret seeks support from his local parish priest as well as a Southern Baptist minister. Regular prayer and seeking spiritual counsel have become an important part of the Baiers' daily routine.

Paul does very well in the capable hands of Dr. Jonas, and a little more than two weeks after this surgery, he walks 3.1 miles in a fundraising event for Children's National.

Eventually Dr. Jonas, one of the best pediatric heart surgeons in the history of this country, retires. He is replaced by Dr. Yves d'Udekem, who will be called upon to perform any additional heart surgeries if Paul requires them. As of this writing, he has performed two additional heart surgeries on Paul. Dr. d'Udekem trained in congenital heart surgery at the Great Ormond Street Hospital for Children in London with the world-renowned Professor Marc de Laval. From there he made a big name for himself at the Royal Children's Hospital in Melbourne, Australia. He joined Children's National Heart Center as division chief of cardiac surgery and codirector of the center in September 2020. He is the Baier Family distinguished professor of cardiac surgery at Children's National, and the Baier family all love and admire him.

꙳

I ASK AMY, who has been the chair of Children's National Hospital Foundation Board for several years and has raised many millions of dollars for the hospital, about her devotion to Paul's care and how she has drawn from that to reach out to other children with similar conditions. "After Paul is born and he is in the cardiac intensive care unit, Bret and I turn to each other and say, 'We have our cause.' And then after his first open-heart surgery, you just can't feel enough gratitude in the world to say thank you. So we really put our weight into trying to make a difference for kids like Paul."

Amy accepts Paul's survival and recovery as a miracle from the time of his first surgery as a newborn, starting with Nurse Kennedy's quick action to get Paul tested. "If we had brought him home from the hospital right away, we would have found him dead in his crib," Amy says. "So we call this nurse our angel because she is so receptive to his color and alerts everyone to it. And as new parents, we don't know if his skin should be pale or not."

While praying with a priest in the hospital for Paul's very first open-heart surgery, Amy has a vision of heaven's beams surrounding Paul on the surgical bed. "And I feel he is going to be okay. I have a lot of visions throughout Paul's health issues, and I always feel God has a plan for Paul and God is protecting him. This is a big part of his healing and his story."

When Amy and Bret are waiting for Paul's first recovery, they talk about "that moment" the surgeon told them about.

When you are in surgery, he had said, you have to stop the heart and then see it restart. "That's the God moment," the surgeon said. "Then I know there's a God."

As time goes by, Bret and Amy think, "Holy cow, we have been through a lot over these years. And it's a miracle that we've gone through." They choose to focus on cultivating an attitude of gratitude, and to see God's purpose even in their hardships.

"I think God gave this to us," Amy says, "because we can hopefully make a small dent or help a few people. And just this morning I am helping someone at Children's Hospital who has a sick kid who needs to get directed to the right doctor. This one has cancer. So I feel like God gave this to us to motivate us so that in our small way we can shine a spotlight for others, and not just for congenital heart disease, but other people hurting. And you realize everyone's experiencing something. You don't always see it or know it. But maybe we can help move the needle in a tiny way. I hope that Paul will continue that.

"And we see that there are these kids in the hospital who don't make it," she adds. "And the question is, why don't they make it, and our son does? And sometimes it's just unexplainable."

Whenever Amy counsels other families who have children who are about to have open-heart surgery, she always tells them to "love on" their child like crazy, and to pray like crazy, because miracles happen.

DESPITE TEN ANGIOPLASTIES and four open-heart surgeries, by age sixteen Paul has grown to over six feet, three inches tall, with a passion for golf like his father. He has had to avoid contact sports, which is a big reason he plays golf. Dr. d'Udekem encourages Paul to get out and exercise, pushing him to run, to engage in regular cardiovascular exercise.

Paul has also learned to self-regulate, monitoring for symptoms so that he can prevent problems from happening. Despite all he's been through, he's sweet and protective of his younger brother, Daniel, and they are very close.

"Paul also is a kid who doesn't want to hold back on life," says Amy. "He likes to go skiing. He likes to go on a roller coaster. We want him to feel normal like a normal kid."

Paul is very advanced for his age. He concentrates on living his life with the attitude that he just doesn't know if he is going to be here tomorrow. He doesn't really like talking about his condition as much as he used to. He wants to focus on the future. He's spoken in front of ballrooms full of people, which his parents consider a miracle in and of itself. But he wants to focus on moving forward in life.

In 2024, however, he has to be a heart patient again.

He goes to a routine appointment at a new place to get checked out for a cold virus or strep, but the extra-cautious doctor there decides to get Paul a chest X-ray. When he looks at the results, he sees a strange shadow. He speculates that it must be from his previous surgery, or some tissue on his lung.

This primary care doctor sends the results to Paul's cardiologist, who says it might be nothing, but decides to check Paul out with an MRI anyway. And so the Baier family goes back to Children's National.

After the MRI, they are sitting there waiting, and six doctors, including Dr. d'Udekem, come in and tell them that Paul has a golf-ball-sized aneurysm just off his heart.

It takes Paul a minute, and he looks at his father with a tear coming down his cheek. "Well, let's do what we've got to do," he says. "Let's knock it out."

Dr. d'Udekem doesn't tell Paul while he's in the room, but he tells Bret that if they don't operate, it could burst, and Paul might not survive more than a few minutes.

The family goes home to think about it overnight. Paul approaches everything with a mature thought process and strong faith. He says, "This is what I have to do and we'll make the most of it and get through it to the other side," which is recovery.

The next day, Bret and Paul play a game of golf at the Burning Tree Club in Bethesda to get their minds off things, and Paul beats his father. Then it's back to the hospital for open-heart surgery—his fifth one.

It goes well, but Paul probably will need to have a sixth surgery at some point. The transplanted parts of his heart continue to need to be replaced as he outgrows them. He may also need more angioplasties. But his doctors think that, because of the advancing technology, they may be able to do any further surgeries without opening up his chest again.

There may need to be surgery if the valve leaks and has to be replaced. Paul's heart is now an adult heart pumping the right way, and they've shored it up to try to prevent any other aneurysms. They still haven't figured out exactly what happened to cause the latest aneurysm, but they are hoping it doesn't happen again.

I wonder about Paul's emotional reaction to all the surgeries and heart procedures.

"He's had surgery at all different ages," Amy says. "I thought this one was the most difficult. He needed more support from friends before we could power him through us, his parents. He never wanted to be perceived as weak as a teenager with his friends and especially girls. And so he just needed the love and support from his friends. And they were amazing. Even though we found out the day before, they had like twenty-five kids that had all put together a video wishing Paul well. His best friend flew into town for one night so he could spend time with him as he recovered."

"He didn't have time to get mentally prepared for it this time," Bret says. "It was just thrown on him. And so it really hit him. I think mortality became more of an issue this time as he was older, thinking about maybe he doesn't make it. And that set in more this time. But he quickly bounced back. He wanted to play golf on the golf team and he was playing really great, as evidenced by beating me the day before the surgery."

After this most recent surgery, Amy calls the doctor who randomly wanted to do a lung X-ray for Paul and tells him, "You just saved my son's life, because had you not done that lung X-ray, chances are he wouldn't have made it." Amy sees this as another divine intervention.

"We wouldn't have seen it," Bret says. "It wouldn't have been spotted and he wouldn't have made it."

"Great doctors like this are the hands of God," Amy says. "They're changing lives."

CHAPTER 2

Damar

IT'S JANUARY 2, 2023, JUST after 9 p.m. in Cincinnati, Ohio. The Buffalo Bills are on the road against the Cincinnati Bengals for *Monday Night Football*. The ABC show is a tradition that goes all the way back to the illustrious announcer Howard Cosell and his bright plaid suits in the 1970s.

Bills safety Damar Hamlin is making a tackle following a completed pass when he takes a hard helmet blow to the chest and goes down, an extremely common event in football.

Hamlin gets back up and takes a few steps, but then collapses straight backward and down to the ground and stops moving.

The stadium's cameras pan to the sidelines and show the suddenly concerned and shocked expression of Dr. Leslie Bisson, chairman of orthopedics at Jacobs School of Medicine in Buffalo, my alma mater, and medical director for both the Buffalo Bills and the Buffalo Sabres ice hockey team. Dr. Bisson oversees an elaborate web of ER docs, emergency responders, and sports orthopedists of both teams who work together and are ready to rush the field at a moment's notice. He has been preparing for this kind of catastrophe for fifteen years, ever since a Buffalo Sabres skater was slashed by a skate to his neck (carotid artery) and nearly bled to death in 2008. After that, he instituted a protocol for both his teams and they frequently rehearse what to do in the event of a cardiac arrest. This protocol has caught on around the NFL. While some sports medicine experts might have thought Dr. Bisson's preparation was an overreaction, he certainly looks prescient tonight.

Cardiologists around the country watching this live see Hamlin fall straight backward and think right away about a drop attack, or cardiac arrest. The medical responders aren't thinking about a diagnosis but rush the field within thirty seconds. "Time is brain" is an adage that neurologists go by, meaning that at times of heart stoppage or insufficient blood flow, brain damage can only be averted if blood flow is restored or CPR is started within a minute or two.

Bills trainer Denny Kellington rushes the field, and as Hamlin's shoulder pads are torn off, he begins CPR within a minute. Dr. Bisson runs over and determines Hamlin has no pulse.

There is an automated external defibrillator (AED) on the field, and the medical team takes the adhesive pads from the machine and places them on Hamlin's chest, and the defibrillator spits out a rhythm. The doctors are horrified to find him in a potentially deadly rhythm, ventricular tachycardia, a wide complex rhythm that won't maintain blood pressure, which deteriorates quickly in this case to ventricular fibrillation, where the heart is simply quivering and not providing oxygen to the brain or vital organs at all.

The team applies a shock to Hamlin's chest, and luckily he returns to normal rhythm and his pulse returns. He remains unconscious. A breathing tube is put down his throat and one of the respiratory therapists pumps air into his lungs via an Ambu bag. He is quickly taken from the field by the response team. They are headed to the University of Cincinnati Medical Center.

ﻙﻟﺑ

SOON AFTER 9 p.m., I begin receiving calls from Fox News to get to my office camera as soon as possible to report on Hamlin's sudden cardiac arrest, the first cardiac arrest during American professional football in fifty-two years. Injuries are common during NFL games, ranging from broken bones all the way up to spinal injuries and potential paralysis, but not cardiac arrests. As I run to my office camera, I wonder how this could have happened, and more importantly, how Damar can possibly recover. There is no reason for me to automatically believe that the extensive team of emergency responders, trainers, and physicians will be able to bring him back to any semblance of normalcy. I know I will be asked in the days and weeks to come whether Damar, if he survives, if he returns to consciousness, will ever be able to play NFL football again, with all its stress and strain.

I can't imagine this night that he will.

On my way to my office camera, I receive a phone call from a brilliant NYU Langone Health cardiologist, Dr. Fred Feit, who hosts for me on *Doctor Radio* on SiriusXM, where I am the medical director. "It's commotio cordis," Feit says. "Damar was hit in the chest at a strange angle with an opposing player's helmet after a tackle and he flopped straight back. He must have had an arrhythmia, ventricular tachycardia, or ventricular fibrillation and they shocked him out of it. There is no doubt about it. Don't let anyone tell you it's anything else."

Because of this discussion with Dr. Feit, I am one of the first to go on TV and mention commotio cordis and explain what it is: a sudden shock to the heart right at that moment of the cardiac cycle when it is repolarizing or returning to its resting state, which Damar himself acknowledges as the cause months later, when all underlying structural heart problems have been ruled out. At the time of the cardiac arrest, this seems strange to say, because it has never happened to a professional football player before.

The heart is a muscle that also generates electric-type impulses from the brain, causing it to contract to pump blood. Dr. Feit explains that commotio cordis occurs when a sharp blow to the chest—at the exact point in the cardiac cycle when it is about to relax—disrupts the cycle and causes the heart to go flaccid. The condition is 97 percent fatal if not treated within three minutes. If treatment is administered in a timely manner, survival rises to 25 percent. Survival rates have been improving by more than 60 percent because of prompt recognition and use of defibrillators. There are about ten to twenty events a year in the US and they generally involve younger athletes than Damar, since their chest muscles aren't as well developed. Commotio cordis also means there is no underlying structural heart disease to explain the heart stopping.

Commotio cordis has been recognized for centuries. As early as the 1700s there were descriptions from the ancient Chinese martial art of Dim Mak ("touch of death"), but the first official commotio cordis report of sudden death was in England in 1898, when a thirteen-year-old cricket batter was struck in the chest by a ball "of moderate velocity." In the twentieth century, commotio cordis events were reported mostly in amateur or professional baseball if a batter was struck in the chest over the heart. This occurrence was and is far more likely than a football helmet causing it during a tackle, especially in professional football, where players have extremely well-developed chest muscles to absorb the blow without transmitting it to the heart. What happened to Damar is extremely unlikely.

It was not until 1995 that recognition of commotio cordis emerged in the general public and physician community as a distinct clinical entity accounting for sudden death in young, healthy athletes and others, thanks to a seminal study in *The New England Journal of Medicine* that reviewed twenty-five cases in children and young adults. Sudden cardiac arrest is the leading cause of death in young athletes but hadn't occurred during an NFL game since the 1950s. Since then there have been rare cases of paralysis, but no cardiac arrests on the field—until Damar.

AT THE HOSPITAL, Dr. Timothy Pritts, chief of surgery and senior trauma surgeon at the University of Cincinnati Health, who, along with 70 million others, saw Damar collapse on TV, is waiting.

He oversees Damar's care from the time of those first tense moments in the hospital. Damar is hooked to a respirator and kept sedated while tests on his heart and brain are run.

Finally, on Wednesday, two days later, Damar wakes up and asks Pritts, "Who won the game?"

Pritts responds, "Damar, you won the game of life."

Pritts tells me in an interview that 150 people are involved in saving Damar. "Football is a team sport; so is trauma. Nurses, ER doctors, a blended cohesive team."

"This is a medical miracle," says Dr. Pritts.

Pritts says it is typical for a patient in this condition to not remember what happened, but Damar remembers "components of it, some of what happened." He remembers the preparation for the game. He remembers being hit and going down. He remembers getting back up.

"Everyone wants to get back on the field," Pritts says. "But there is no way to predict it within the first week."

Dr. Pritts has worked on many amazing recoveries over the years. "One patient had a hatchet to the chest, another hatchet to the back, which went through the internal mammary artery, and had four cardiac arrests over twenty-four hours but fully recovered. But Damar has as much courage and fortitude as anyone. This is a very important factor."

Pritts says that an event like this raises awareness so that many more people learn CPR and every sports complex has an AED.

The University of Cincinnati Medical Center takes care of over 5,000 trauma patients per year and is the only Level 1 trauma center in the region. Pritts is extremely proud of his great team there.

After a few days in Cincinnati, Damar is brought back to Buffalo, where he is admitted to the hospital for a few days and then undergoes extensive outpatient rehabilitation under the watchful guidance of Dr. Bisson. In February, Damar makes a spectacular on-field appearance at the Super Bowl.

At this point, few believe that Damar will play football again.

علم

DR. BISSON DOESN'T visit Damar in the hospital in Cincinnati. Instead he travels home with the team. But he visits Damar in the hospital in Buffalo multiple times.

When he first sees Damar, he gives him a huge hug. "It's very hard not to get emotional when something like this happens to one of these guys because we take care of them," says Dr. Bisson. "They trust us. We know them very well. It's really challenging. I can't hug him enough. I hug him ten times over the next week or so. And then my wife hugs him, too at the Super Bowl. They invite us all out to celebrate that things have worked out so well. She sees Damar for the first time ever and she hugs him too."

Bisson realizes how challenging Damar's recovery is. Football basically causes him to die, and when he is revived, he vows to return. "It speaks to the love he has for the game. It is a show of great courage."

Dr. Pritts and Dr. Bisson agree that Damar is a great human being. "He is already laughing and joking from the time he wakes up in the hospital," Dr. Bisson says. "In Cincinnati, as in Buffalo, he is showing his gratitude to God for having survived." Dr. Pritts says, "He wants to give back now. He has created a fellowship for ten different people to go to better area hospitals within the Catholic school system."

In the wake of his cardiac arrest, Damar also focuses his efforts on CPR awareness and becomes a spokesperson for the American Heart Association. Dr. Bisson has been obsessed for decades with bringing CPR training to Buffalo's underserved communities. Now is his best opportunity to really get it to happen.

"There's a real national and community disparity in terms of who gets bystander CPR on the street," says Dr. Bisson. "I am working with my department to try to help overcome this here in Buffalo. Damar is working nationally on the same thing. We have athletic trainers that deliver training services to public schools. And a lot of them are in historically underserved communities."

Damar's foundation has raised millions of dollars, which he's using to supply AEDs to underserved communities. His foundation recently supplied an AED to every public school in Utah. Meanwhile, Bisson says he and his faculty in Buffalo have trained over 7,000 community members in CPR in the last year.

Bisson tells me that the chances of having an out-of-the-hospital cardiac arrest and even surviving is only 10 percent. A bystander knowing CPR increases your chances, and it is made even higher "if you have an AED that's available and you get a shock to the patient within a minute."

Bisson feels very fortunate that he and the team had been practicing for a cardiac arrest for over a decade even while believing it was very unlikely to actually ever happen. His team rehearses for a variety of things: collapsed lungs and hemothorax (blood in the lungs) and injuries to the spine that cause paralysis. Sometimes players are knocked unconscious, and sometimes one will have a seizure on the field. So twice every year, Dr. Bisson and his team go through a series of rescue scenarios.

He considers his trainers to be the real heroes because of the work they do with the players to get them ready for the games. "You need a plan," he says. "We are all on the same page with a standardized plan that we practice and review and then submit to the league. Experts look at it. And then we rehearse it, and we review the plan before every game."

The NFL is very well resourced. Each team has an airway management physician and an emergency response physician, both of whom are emergency medicine trained. During NFL games, players often get hit and go down, and sometimes they'll get right back up after a few minutes and run off the field. If the injury looks serious, however, these teams are ready to rush onto the field as the player stays down.

"We recognize pretty quickly in Damar's situation that something is different. I am one of the first responders. I see he is having agonal breathing and is unresponsive. So the cardiac arrest training scenario automatically kicks in. We have practiced it and we are ready. As soon as we say, 'Hey we got a guy in an arrest situation,' everybody runs out." There are four doctors and several emergency personnel on the field in a matter of seconds. Dr. Bisson is in charge when it's a Bills player, and Cincinnati is in charge when it's theirs. So in Damar's case, it is Bisson who is in charge.

"We radio to everybody. Hey, all hands on deck. They come out. We pretty quickly get his helmet and his equipment off, and start administering CPR, and get the defibrillator, put the pads on him, shock him, and get a cardiac rhythm back."

Bisson says that it is he and the head athletic trainer who get Damar's helmet off. Someone starts Ambu bagging him, which means breathing for him with a handheld device. "Somebody starts doing chest compressions, and somebody is cutting off his equipment. Gives us a place to apply the defibrillator pads."

I ask Bisson how long it takes to get the shoulder pads off. "You can get them off pretty fast if you have trauma scissors. You just sort of cut right up the center."

Bisson's medical staff travels with the team and they know every player well, even their medical histories, but in an emergency like a cardiac arrest, Bisson automatically defers to emergency responders with more expertise. "We all understand our roles. So if a guy's got a broken leg, I'm your man. I'm going to straighten it out." When he sees Damar go down, he recognizes right away that it's a cardiac emergency and he calls for more emergency help.

Dr. Bisson says there's no reason to believe that NFL athletes are somehow immune to cardiac arrests. "There have been a couple of cardiac arrests in the NHL. And there have been cardiac arrests in the NBA. So cardiac arrests are definitely a thing that has happened before in professional sports."

Still, Dr. Bisson says he had never seen anything as dramatic as Damar's case before, "and I hope to never see it again."

Besides Damar, Dr. Bisson has been involved in two situations that he would call miraculous. Another Buffalo Bills player broke his neck on the field in 2007 and, with immediate treatment with iced saline (considered controversial) and rapid surgical stabilization with fusion, "almost completely recovered, which if you have complete paralysis, then you don't get that back. It's practically unheard-of. He is now walking. He had a complete spinal cord injury with no sensory or motor function immediately after the injury."

The other miracle case involved Richard Zednik, in early 2008. A hockey player for the Buffalo Sabres, Zednik was slashed in the neck with a skate and had a carotid artery laceration, which can lead to death within two minutes. But because it happened at a professional hockey game, Dr. Bisson was ready to jump down from the stands as the team doctor and jam his fingers into Zednik's neck and keep the pressure on the carotid artery for many minutes. Zednik was raced to the hospital and up to the operating room, and he received several units of blood. Not only did he live, but he was perfectly fine and went back to playing hockey.

It was Zednik's miracle recovery that led Bisson to push for the extensive preparation and emergency protocols that ultimately led to the miracle save of Hamlin sixteen years later.

Dr. Bisson and his team have won several awards for the successful recovery of Damar Hamlin, including one from the American Heart Association. In July 2023, the Bills medical and training staff received the Pat Tillman Award for service at the ESPY Awards for the lifesaving measures they performed on Damar Hamlin.

☙

IN APRIL 2023, only a few months after his cardiac arrest, several specialists gave Damar clearance to resume playing football. He went back to playing that fall, and has had an impressive NFL career since.

Dr. Bisson says that he isn't completely surprised by Damar's full recovery, but he calls it a medical miracle. After all, Damar is a high-performance professional athlete who wasn't expected to have a cardiac arrest. He had an extremely unusual one, and managed to recover to the point where he could play professional football again.

Dr. Bisson calls football players a different breed of human beings: "These guys do not slow down. They're always trying to run faster. They're almost a kind of a class of superhuman. We all know in sports medicine, when we take care of the professional athletes they get different injuries than everybody else. They recover faster than everybody else."

But even given their super recuperative powers," Dr. Bisson says, "which helps to explain Damar's recovery in part, it is even more amazing to consider that he survives completely intact. The 10 percent figure for survival after out-of-the-hospital cardiac arrest doesn't include the fact that most survivors have ongoing permanent neurological or cardiac damage due to insufficient blood flow during the event, damage which Damar lacks. He is back on the field. Therein lies the greatest miracle.

"At the end of the day, you want a person not just to survive a cardiac arrest, but to survive like Damar does, to be normal and fine afterwards. That is, you can keep someone alive with CPR, but the faster you get electricity to them and shock their heart back into a normal rhythm, the more normal their brain is going to be."

"A lot of it is thanks to you," I tell him. "You're a great doctor."

"Oh, I don't know about that," he replies. "I'm just a guy who is doing this job."

CHAPTER 3

Breakthrough

THE WATER OF LAKE ST. LOUIS hardly ever freezes over, which means it is quite the unusual event when thick ice covers it during Martin Luther King Jr. weekend, 2015.

Fourteen-year-old John Smith, an eighth grader in Christian Middle School outside of St. Louis, has just won a school basketball tournament and visits the lake at night with his friends, Josh Sander and Josh Rieger.

The boys are throwing rocks at the ice, picking up the heaviest things that all three of them can lift, and throwing them onto the ice, trying to get it to crack.

But it does not crack, and they notice that it is very thick. Then, almost like a dare, one of them ventures out onto the ice. Soon all three of them end up on the ice, listening to music, getting as close to the edge of it as they can, and sliding on their bellies like penguins.

When Josh Rieger's older sister, Jamie, finds out about this later that night, she is very curious about the lake and how they managed to go out onto the ice without it cracking. So the next day, on a dare from her, they all go back to the lake. It is warmer, in the low 40s, but the ice is still there, slowly melting.

As they try to get back on, they know they are taking a big risk.

The ice feels thinner, less stable. Then John gets a call from his mother, asking when he wants her to pick him up. As he speaks with her on the phone, he distractedly walks around, getting closer to the edge of the ice.

Finishing the call, his mom ends with "I love you."

"I love you too," John replies.

Within seconds, John falls through the ice. He is instantly shocked as dirty, murky water goes up his nose and even into his contact lenses.

Screams echo across the ice. Three boys are in the water. Josh Rieger is closest to John, both about twenty-five to fifty feet from the shore. Meanwhile, Josh Sander is much closer to the dock, and Jamie Reiger is on the shore and is screaming for help. The two other boys are screaming too. The ice breaks up, and Josh Rieger is hanging on to a piece of ice, hoping he can stay afloat long enough to be rescued. John pushes Josh Rieger up so he can hang on to the ice as long as possible, but then John loses consciousness.

A rescue crew, led by Wentzville Fire Protection District Captain Tommy Shine, is on the scene within minutes. Josh Sander is out of the water and the team is able to pull Josh Rieger out. But John Smith is still under the water.

Shine immediately gets on his wet suit and goes out to

look for John. At this point, John has been under the water for ten minutes already.

Shine carries a twelve-foot pike pole to attach to John's clothing and pull him out when and if he finds him. As he goes along the ice, Shine hears a familiar voice calling from the shore, directing him where to go. When Shine looks to see who is calling to him, no one is there.

As he pokes the ice with his pike pole, he finally finds an area with less resistance, and sees John's shirt. He pulls him from the water, but John is unresponsive, not breathing, and he has no pulse. His skin is gray.

CPR is started and the EMTs breathe air into his lungs through an Ambu bag.

They are unable to bring him back.

The ambulance arrives and brings John to nearby St. Joseph Hospital. Dr. Kent Sutterer, an ER physician, is the first to see John on arrival. He is not breathing, with no heart sounds, and his skin temperature is so cold it is incompatible with life. John has zero neurological signs. No signs that he will have any kind of life even if Dr. Sutterer's team is able to start his heart again. He is flatlined dead for more than fifty minutes.

"He is gone," thinks Dr. Sutterer.

Meanwhile, John's mother, Joyce, gets a call and thinks it must be time to pick him up. Instead she's told that he has been pulled from the lake and doesn't have a heartbeat. She immediately leaves for the hospital.

When she arrives, they won't let her see John right away. While she's waiting in a small room, a nun named Sister

Donna comes in and sees her crying. "She starts praying and suddenly the most awesome peace comes over me," says Joyce.

Then they allow her in to see John. There are no fewer than thirty people working on him in the room. She can see on the machine behind him that he is still flatlined.

Yet they make every attempt to save him. Keith Terry, an emergency medical technician and future firefighter, is in the ER that day. When John comes in, Terry and other ER staff perform CPR, but there is no rhythm for them to shock. They give him epinephrine and warm him up with blankets and fluids. They intubate him, attach him to the respirator. Still, Terry says he has never seen anything like this before. "I have a feeling his name is John when he comes in the door. I call him John without knowing if it is really his name or not. Like John Doe. I talk to him while I'm doing CPR and say, 'Come on, let's go, John!' I see this lifeless boy and I said, 'Come on, you got this!'"

Dr. Sutterer says that his usual practice is to only administer CPR for ten minutes. "Survivability after ten minutes is close to zero. But about once a month I keep codes going for longer until I pronounce death. This one with Smith is a cold-water drowning, and cold water can keep the organs viable longer. The clock doesn't really start ticking until a body is warmed up to room temp, and with Smith we start the clock when he goes from 88 to 96."

The team is getting everything in place to warm John. They use a special medical form of blow dryers, as well as warm IV fluid, to get his body back up to normal temp.

One of Dr. Sutterer's colleagues says to him, "I know they're not dead until they're warm and dead." That is their approach, but still, his temperature rises to 95 and time keeps passing with no pulse. Meaningful recovery from here is unheard-of.

Dr. Sutterer also decides to provide treatment for longer than normal because John is fourteen, and because of his mom. "I want parents to see we've done everything we can and have made extraordinary efforts. My plan is to tell her that John is dead. When she gets there, I say as gently as I can that her son is gone, and he isn't coming back."

Joyce feels desperate, and prays, "God, you can't take him from me. It took me seventeen years to get him." (John was adopted.) Having been involved in Bible study, Joyce knows the power of God's words and believing in them. "So, I pray, please, God, give me back my son."

"Joyce starts praying," Dr. Sutterer says, "and things change in the room. There is a presence in the room you can feel."

"I feel that God is in the room with us," Terry says. "His mom is praying and praying. She says, 'Lord, don't take my son. Dear Lord, bring your presence into this room right now.'"

It has been well over an hour since John went into the water. It is very rare that a treatment runs this long, but something keeps Dr. Sutterer from stopping. John's mother keeps praying, and lifts up one last big prayer.

Suddenly, there is a pulse.

"We feel a pulse," Terry says. "He is back."

Dr. Sutterer says the event is extraordinary in many ways. "This just doesn't happen . . . It's an absolute miracle. I have zero explanation. I have never seen this before in my career. I've seen people come back after a few minutes. But after coding someone for an hour? Never in my career. We give him lots of epinephrine, which kick-starts the heart in cardiac arrest. Sometimes we stimulate the heart with medicine—chemicals make the heart beat, but that doesn't mean you have blood flow to the brain and it doesn't mean you have meaningful survival. I am not expecting him to wake up from here. Also, he didn't get cold enough fast enough to think we have preserved his brain function. So we never expect him to wake up after this. I feel if we even get twelve or twenty-four hours of life after his pulse comes back, it will be a miracle."

Studies have shown that the amount of time doing CPR leading to favorable neurological outcomes is generally less than thirty minutes, except in extremely unusual cases.

According to an article published in the *Annals of Emergency Medicine* in 1998, "Victims of cold water near-drowning have been documented to survive prolonged (up to 66 minutes) cold water submersion with little or no neurologic deficit. In these cases, the length of effective anoxia is often much longer than that usually required to produce irreversible neurologic damage. This remarkable protection of the brain is commonly attributed to (1) very low rectal temperatures (T_{re}), which are presumed to provide neurologic protection by lowering cerebral metabolic requirements for oxygen ($CMRO_2$); and (2) the mammalian dive reflex, which is presumed to optimize the delivery of limited available oxygen stores to the brain."

In other words, in cold water the body shifts into a protective mechanism by increasing oxygen flow to the brain while at the same time oxygen requirements are lower at colder temperatures. This protective physiology is working on John Smith's behalf to some extent, but the time submerged in the cold water is only fifteen minutes, while the amount of time in cardiac arrest outside the water is over an hour, unheard-of in terms of a full neurological recovery.

Overall, expectations for John, even when his pulse comes back, remain extremely low. Restoring his full brain function after this prolonged a heart stoppage outside the water would be unprecedented.

John is airlifted to Children's Hospital in the downtown area. When Joyce arrives and meets with the doctor there, he says to her, "His heart is beating now, but how far do you want us to go to save your son?"

Joyce stands up and says, "You do what you know how to do, and my God will do what he does."

Meanwhile, medical staff are already cross-matching John's heart for another boy who needs a heart; they don't think John will make it through the night. But John *does* make it through. He is on a ventilator. Then his fever spikes and his lungs need to be drained.

While Joyce keeps praying, the story gets out. People all over the world are praying.

"I REMEMBER WAKING up in the hospital and staring at the ceiling," John Smith says to me in an interview. "And I remember a couple of things. My uncle Don. I remember him being there and holding my hand. And then I remember a pastor that I grew up with; his name is Mark Shepherd. I remember him asking me a series of questions. He asks me if I remember meeting with him earlier that year. I say yes, and then he asks if I remember who I am. I say yes, and then he asks if he is still good-looking, and I say no."

It is John's third day in the hospital when he wakes up. He says he doesn't remember anything from when he was asleep, but when he wakes up he is completely oriented. "I have no idea what has happened to me. I know I have fallen in the ice. My mom explains that to me. I don't know anything past that."

A week later, John is moved to the transition unit, and a week after that, he walks out and goes home. He doesn't realize the extent of his miracle right away.

"I grew up very religious," John says. "My church is Assemblies of God. I spent most of my childhood in the church. I can honestly say, though, that I was not saved at the time that I fell in the water, which is why I truly believe that I didn't feel an afterlife experience."

John says that after he wakes up in the hospital, he doesn't have a breakthrough experience right away. In fact, at first he feels angry, wondering why he gets a second chance when billions of others on the planet don't. It isn't until he is a sophomore in high school that "one night I really just confess, and the breakthrough starts."

John's mother brings the story to the renowned Reverend Samuel Rodriguez ("Pastor Sam"), who has become a mentor to John. Pastor Sam brings the story to Dr. Oz's television show, and soon a movie called *Breakthrough* is conceived, with Pastor Sam as the executive producer.

"I'm very, very blessed," John says. "This story has done amazing things, and seeing the impact that it has on people's lives and their ability to believe is more rewarding than any amount of money or any amount of fame. People witness God through this story and it inspires them to miracles in their own lives."

The movie is about John Smith's spiritual breakthrough years later, but it is also about breaking through the ice of a deep lake to retrieve a teen and resuscitate him at the hospital where by all estimates he is already dead.

Pastor Sam and John become fast friends. Pastor Sam has a degree from Lehigh University in organizational psychology, which helps him navigate between different worlds. "I grew up as an evangelical Christian in Bethlehem, Pennsylvania. My dad was a Mack truck worker," he says in an interview.

In addition to his church ministry, Pastor Sam works as a movie producer and as an advisor to US presidents (including George W. Bush, Obama, Trump, Biden). He has an easy, comforting manner that is at once spiritual and fraternal, warm yet ethereal. "Just like Samuel in the Old Testament. I'm not a David; I'm a Samuel. My assignment is to find the Davids and equip them, to speak hope and faith into the Davids and tell them, Go defeat the giants. Go confront the giants of your generation. Integrity and love change the world."

Pastor Sam says, "Knowing God is about having the humility to call upon a force greater than yourself. John Smith's mother knew to do this. I know to do it, to lift up my hands and say, God, I need you to get this, I can't do this without you. God answers prayers on so many occasions."

John's story has inspired many people to grow in their faith, including Pastor Sam as well as those who were there to help John the day he fell through the ice. Dr. Sutterer, a faithful and devout Christian, says, "My faith is strengthened by my experience with John. God performs miracles when he chooses to."

CHAPTER 4

The Albert Schweitzer of Sudan

DR. TOM CATENA IS PREPARING for surgery in his primitive operating room in the 450-bed Mother of Mercy Hospital, in the heart of the Nuba Mountains of Sudan. The hospital was founded by a Catholic archbishop of the diocese of El Obeid. It is the only hospital for three hundred miles.

Bullets fly frequently in this area, and the population of close to a million people lives and hides in caves, without running water. It is a war-torn region, and whereas the rest of Africa has developed its civilization, the Nuba Mountains have not. Water wells are targeted by the government, and the locals are forced to bore holes into temporary rivers for water. Today there is a moment of quiet, as if God himself is watching Dr. Catena operate, and is superimposing a period of silence.

The patient is Rita, a three-year-old girl who came to Dr. Catena with a bulging abdomen, after trekking with her mother for six hours through the mountains to arrive here. Dr. Catena swept an ultrasound wand across her belly and discovered, to his horror, that one of Rita's kidneys was completely obliterated by cancer, and the other was almost halfway gone, with the tumor (by appearance probably a Wilms tumor) creeping its way toward the northern pole of the kidney.

Rita's mother is very calm, especially given her circumstances—not only does her daughter have cancer, but they have been living in a cave to avoid artillery shelling from the Sudan government.

Catena is the only surgeon for over a million people, and operates on over two thousand patients per year (with nine hundred of them being major cases), but he has never been formally trained in surgery. And he looks at this particular case of kidney cancer with absolute terror.

من

I FIRST MET Dr. Catena at a Friday night Shabbat dinner in 2023, hosted by Rabbi Erica Gerson. She and her husband, Mark, are philanthropists and big supporters of Catena's work, through an organization known as African Mission Healthcare. I was looking forward to meeting him and I immediately recognized him from his photo—bald; bushy, expressive eyebrows; unshaven, with a bright white-toothed smile that must be difficult to maintain, I thought, in such a rural place as Sudan.

Because of his medical missionary work, Dr. Catena has

been called a modern-day Albert Schweitzer—who was a medical missionary to Africa in the twentieth century and won the Nobel Peace Prize in 1952.

For someone as esteemed as Dr. Catena, I wasn't expecting his humility. No posturing, just an easy smile, a manner that all patients hope for. He exuded a healing aura, almost as though healing were a cream you could apply. His wife, Nasima, a Sudanese nurse, wasn't there at the dinner, but I could tell from photos that she is also calm and easygoing. The couple has two adopted children from the region, a six-year-old and a baby. The older child attends school in a small one-story hut near the hospital while their mother works with their father on lifesaving work. The child's education is augmented with homeschooling in both Arabic and English.

Over the course of the dinner, Dr. Catena sat in the middle of the room and talked with everyone. I overheard him asking other people about their lives, rather than focusing too much on his own work. When it was my turn, it was clear that he knew who I was, and he was fully engaged talking with me about my medical practice as well as my journalistic work. The whole room listened raptly to Dr. Catena whenever he responded to questions about his arduous work at the hospital.

مطب

CATENA TELLS ME in an interview that he believes in medical miracles, which he defines in his world as an outcome that is totally unexpected based on very limited resources and skills. "The fact that we can stay open here is a miracle. Over sixteen years, there has been a staff revolt, we have been bombed twice, there have been incredible challenges, problems from staff [expatriates from Kenya] refusing to work."

Catena is a graduate of my alma mater, Brown University, with a bachelor's degree in mechanical engineering, which he now says prepared him to work with scant supplies and invent creative solutions. Catena describes himself as a "cradle Catholic," and after college he became involved with the evangelical Christian group Campus Crusade for Christ (now known as Cru), which spurred his interest in medicine. He earned a medical degree from Duke. He went on to become a navy flight surgeon, and he also trained in family practice.

From the beginning of medical school he fully intended to use his training for medical missionary work.

Beginning in 1999, he began to work in Africa, first in Mutomo, Kenya, and then at St. Mary's Mission Hospital in Nairobi. Catena never intended to stay so long, but the challenging work and the enormous medical need of the populations consumed him and motivated him to stay. He moved to Gidel, Sudan, in 2008 to become the only full-time doctor there. Most of Dr. Catena's surgeries have involved treating gunshot victims and trying to stop the bleeding and repair the damage before the patient dies. Over the years he has managed to save many more lives than he has lost.

When Catena first arrived in Sudan in 2008, there were fifteen people working at the Mother of Mercy Hospital, Dr. Jon Fielder, cofounder of African Mission Healthcare, told Fox News Digital in a recent interview from Kenya. (I met Fielder at Gerson's Shabbat dinner table too.) He told Fox Digital about the great contrast between what the hospital looked like when it opened in 2008 and now. The staff on opening day at Catena's hospital consisted of "a couple of Catholic nuns and Tom and about a dozen local staff," Fielder said. Now they have 270 staff, and over 50 of them are formally trained as health workers. "It's really incredible. There's a local training school there for students to become physician assistants and midwives."

Catena's hospital is also supported by the Catholic Medical Mission Board and the Sudan Relief Fund. What started out as an eighty-bed facility now treats up to four hundred patients a day. Giving up the comforts of the Western world, Catena lives in a small hut adjacent to the hospital so he can respond to emergencies at night. Every year the hospital treats up to 75,000 patients and he performs 1,500 surgeries. They treat malaria, tuberculosis, leprosy, fractures, kids with brain conditions, and they perform adult and pediatric surgery.

Yet, Mother of Mercy Hospital still utilizes water pumped from a local riverbed, and though the hospital does have antibiotics and intravenous lines, it relies on two old-fashioned autoclaves with steam to sterilize equipment. No one in the US has used this type of equipment in several decades. Catena improvises with a huge cylindrical kettle and a stove filled with charcoal. For anesthesia he either uses spinal anesthesia or, for general anesthesia for more extensive surgeries, utilizes a vaporizer, filled with halothane, and a set of bellows to blow the halothane over the patient. He induces anesthesia with ketamine, keeps patients paralyzed with succinyl choline, and then uses the halothane to keep them asleep. Three nurses help him with the primitive anesthesia while he operates. He has an Oxford miniature anesthetic vaporizer, which he says looks like an "espresso machine." The hospital has a limited lab for basic chemistries and blood counts, an X-ray machine, and the ultrasound. The hospital is powered by solar panels and a backup generator. In his home, Dr. Catena does not have running water, which means he has no bathroom or shower, not even a flush toilet.

مطر

AS DR. CATENA is getting ready for surgery for Rita, he is assisted by a friend, another family practitioner, Dr. Corry Chapman, who is visiting the hospital from Washington, DC, for a month. The two doctors put on cloth gowns and latex gloves while the equipment is laid out on the surgical table, freshly sterilized by the autoclave. The vaporizer is running and filled with halothane, ready to be pumped out by the bellows into a small cloud over Rita.

Rita looks at Dr. Catena, and their eyes connect, a transference of trust between them. Her short life has been extremely hard. He is her only hope. He is deeply motivated by his faith and his passion for his patients. He will do his best, but he does not think he can save her and isn't really even sure how to go about it.

Though he has taken out a whole kidney before, he has never removed part of one, a process that is far more difficult because it involves removing the tumor while leaving as much healthy kidney tissue as possible. And though he has removed a kidney for a likely Wilms tumor in a child, he has also never worked on both kidneys at the same time.

His only guidance is coming from an instructional YouTube video in Polish (a language he does not speak) that describes this kind of surgery in children with kidney cancer. He still can't really believe he was able to access this particular video. He was preparing for the case with Dr. Chapman and they were looking for guidance and Chapman suggested an online search. But Dr. Catena knew this was likely futile because the internet almost never worked in the Nuba Mountains, and when it did, it was very slow. In fact, it hadn't worked in many weeks.

Still, Dr. Chapman suggested, "Let's check on YouTube to see if we can figure out how to do this surgery." And so the two doctors got down on their hands and knees and prayed to God for the internet. And then, miraculously, the internet came on, and they quickly found the Polish instruction video. They could just make out the blurred images of the Polish doctors and the young child they were operating on. They carefully looked at the equipment being used and the techniques employed during the operation. They were able to glean the basics, though they lacked more than half of the tools the surgeons were using, including an ice slurry. Then, just as the video finished playing, the internet connection went down and they couldn't get it back.

Dr. Catena keeps replaying the video in his mind as he prepares to operate. He prays for little Rita's survival.

"God fills in the gaps beyond what I can do," he says to himself.

He feels anxious, worrying about his ability to accomplish the goal of the operation, which is the complete resection of all the cancerous tissue. He will need to determine where on the left kidney to cut, since only the lower third appears to be cancerous. This is what he needed the YouTube video for the most. He thinks he can tell visually where the normal tissue ends and the cancer starts, but what if he guesses wrong? If he gauges this line correctly and manages to save the part of the left kidney that isn't enveloped in cancer, a cure might be obtainable. But can he get this young patient safely through the operation? What if the bleeding is so bad that it cannot be controlled?

Catena attends mass every day and prays for success and guidance. Today, before the surgery, he prays particularly hard for Rita.

❧

ONE OF DR. Catena's nurses flaps the bellows, and Rita is enveloped in halothane. Dr. Catena can envision every anesthesiologist in the US cringing at this antiquated technique, and yet here it is successful. Rita is unconscious and her vital signs are stable, and the operation begins. Dr. Catena removes his scalpel from its sheath, confident that it has been well sterilized by his autoclave set over hot coals, and makes his first incision into the tiny girl's abdomen. He is lucky to have Dr. Chapman assisting him in the surgery, though he too is a family practitioner, not a surgeon. Dr. Catena longs for the sense of relief he will feel when the surgery is finally finished and he is closing the abdomen. But there are hours to go before he reaches this point.

Surgery is performed one careful cut and tie after another. Dr. Catena cannot get ahead of himself. It is like he is driving a car through fog, where he can see just ahead but never all the way down the road. He only reaches his destination safely if every step is careful and deliberate.

Wilms tumors (also called nephroblastomas) are only found in both kidneys 5 percent of the time. And when the tumor is this extensive, the chance of long-term survival is only above 50 percent with expert surgery followed by radiation and chemotherapy. Even in rural regions this survival rate is achievable provided that there is proper surgical, chemo, and radiation treatment, and Catena does not have radiation therapy at his disposal.

Rita's tumor is so extensive that Catena is almost positive that it must have spread up the renal vein by the time he gets to it. He prays that he is wrong.

Three hours into the surgery, Catena and Chapman are working well even though they have never operated together before and neither of them are surgeons. Catena cuts through the skin, the visceral fat, while Chapman trails him and ties off bleeders. Chapman uses primitive retractors to help keep the kidneys visible and accessible to Catena. Nurses continually wash out the surgical field. But the bleeding is substantial for such a tiny patient, and Catena worries that he won't have enough transfused blood to give her.

He removes the lower part of the left kidney first, the more difficult part of the operation. He hopes he has taken all the cancerous tissue, but he can only estimate it. He doesn't have the ability to send pathology to a laboratory in the middle of the operation (known as a fresh frozen section) and wait for the result to make sure the margins are clear. Once he has finished with the left kidney and stopped the excessive bleeding and made sure that the sutures are holding, Catena turns to the right kidney, which he removes in its entirety, a procedure he has done before.

Rita makes it. In a moment of great emotion, she wakes up in recovery and smiles up at her mother and the other members of her family who crowd around the bed. Catena has tears in his eyes. He says it is the greatest medical miracle he has ever been involved with. "It is not my skill by any stretch. It is clear that God helps us here. His presence is more apparent in this type of situation, much more raw, stark; we rely much more on the grace of God and God's providence."

After the surgery, Rita develops pneumonia and is in the hospital's rudimentary ICU for several days as the follow-up chemotherapy is withheld for weeks. Then she rallies, as Dr. Catena holds his breath, and she recovers. "I am not a faith healer," Catena says. "But this is the most miraculous case that I have ever witnessed or been a part of. This kind of case is why I do this. In an underserved area, with minimal resources, with particularly difficult cases where the patient has nowhere else to go, where they don't have another option, we can provide them a service to give them a chance, but we also rely on God for a positive outcome."

Two years after the surgery, even without half of the chemo she is supposed to get and none of the radiation therapy, Rita is still doing well without recurrence of the cancer. The remaining piece of her left kidney has grown to compensate, and her kidney function has returned toward normal. Catena says that at four years after the operation, at the age of seven, she continues to do well. Her life is very difficult, but at least she has a life. "Rita's case in particular is why I do what I do," Catena says. "The reward is there when the patient survives. It is the only reward necessary."

Catena has rarely operated on kidneys and had never taken out part of one before. "We are able to take the right kidney out and leave in forty percent of the left. Making it through the surgery is one miracle. Getting in and out of her home area without being shelled is another. Fully recovering is a third major miracle."

‮⁂‬

CATENA TELLS ME that faith is the reason for his success. Even with all the improvements in terms of personnel and supplies, "we are pretty bare-bones." He says he experiences medical miracles at his hospital all the time. I am amazed to learn that he performs allographic skin grafts (taken from the patient's own skin), and he tells me about one twenty-year-old who had a seizure, fell into the fire, sustained full-thickness burns over 50 percent of his body, but was then treated and cured by Catena with skin grafts.

It is clear to me that he is driven by his strong, overriding faith. His work is exhausting, often twelve hours or more per day, as he responds to tragedy and desperation. Through it all, Catena feels the presence of God. His success rate is very high given the difficult circumstances. While the Nuba Mountains are not situated directly in the middle of the larger civil war in Sudan, there is still substantial fighting there. And Catena, as the main doctor for the hospital, does everything from delivering babies to removing bullets. He tells me he sees a lot of dysentery from the local people drinking water from the river that hasn't been purified or boiled first. There is also a great deal of malnutrition and famine.

Catena says that God is in charge there and is looking after him and the people. He is driven by faith, compassion for his patients, and an overriding commitment to their health.

In 2024, Dr. Catena wins a completely unexpected award: the NCAA Theodore Roosevelt Award, which honors a former All-American football player (nose guard) who has gone on to great accomplishments beyond football. Catena credits sports for teaching teamwork and perseverance, traits that have helped him over and over again as he battles through the night trying to save wounded or infected soldiers or local citizens. He has also won the 2017 Aurora Prize for Awakening Humanity, the 2018 Catholics in Media Associates Social Justice Award, the 2018 Catholic Doctor of the Year, and the 2020 Gerson L'Chaim Prize for Outstanding Christian

Medical Missionary Service. Through it all, he continues to work as a volunteer without pay. And though Dr. Catena has been recognized internationally—and repeatedly—for humanitarian service, it is in Gidel, Sudan, that he is recognized the most, as a local hero. He is the only doctor working permanently in the Nuba Mountains, the only doctor available around the clock, the only doctor who stayed when all the other humanitarian organizations left as the war heated up. His dedication to the people of the region is unwavering. He says simply, "If I leave, people will die." As one surgeon, Dr. James Peck, who has covered for Catena several times, says, "Tom is extremely committed to giving the best possible care to every patient."

علم

IT IS SAD to consider that, once saved from her condition, Rita has to return to a world of suffering in this war-torn country. Like several of the chapters of this book that take place in vastly underserved areas, the miracles stand out more here than when advanced technology enables them. Catena is compelled to perform many different kinds of surgeries he was never trained to do. Mother of Mercy Hospital is the only trauma center within a three-hundred-mile radius. Patients have been known to walk for many days to be treated here. One father pulled his son in a wagon for one hundred fifty miles to find lifesaving help here for his child.

Catena has participated in many other miracles, though he considers Rita to be the greatest. He tells me more about the twenty-year-old epileptic man named Samson who kept falling into the fire each time the flickering lights provoked a seizure. He came to Catena with severe third-degree burns over half his body. "His condition was really bad, and his skin was as hard as a rock. We felt there was no way this guy could survive even at a US burn center. Here he had to go to just a general ward where it's a hundred and four degrees and there are flies everywhere."

Catena started to debride the wounds, cleaning and cutting off dead tissue over a two-month period. He did several skin grafts, taking them from all over the body. "At first he couldn't get out of bed, and when he did, his skin would crack, and it was very painful. The nurses did all the work, and slowly, he recovered. Now all of his skin has healed, and he is doing well on antiseizure drugs."

The final miracle Catena describes to me involved Kuku (which means firstborn), who was nine months old when he came to the hospital in the summer of 2011. "The civil war had started. Our staff at the time was made up of local people and expatriates, including nurses, midwives, and lab people. But when the war started, they all left, including my anesthesiologist. Unfortunately, the day they all left, a truckload of civilians came in who had been hit with bombs from the war."

Baby Kuku came in with an obstruction of the intestine (intussusception), which can be fatal if not treated. Kuku was vomiting; he had bloody diarrhea. If the intestine is obstructed too long, it dies, and the child dies. Dr. Catena was terrified when he saw this because he knew Kuku needed surgery and he had to put him to sleep and insert a breathing tube. But the anesthesiologist had left.

He had never done intubation before, and he knew it would be far more difficult on a young child. But Kuku's condition was getting worse and worse, and he was very dehydrated.

"I had no choice but to take him into surgery," Catena said. "A nurse was assisting me. I got the tube down the trachea—and saw his tiny lungs inflating. I found I had been holding my own breath and started breathing again. I inflated the bag and was breathing air into his lungs myself. Finally, a nurse took it over, and I was able to operate. I opened the abdomen, saw a dead bowel, resected the intestine, and stitched it back together. He woke up and did great. He is now fourteen years old."

Despite his amazing prowess, Catena knows his limitations. Kuku was an almost impossible case. Catena had never anesthetized a patient before. He didn't have professional staff there. Even under the best of circumstances, Kuku might not have made it. "But he did with God's help."

Dr. Catena is not alone in Nuba. He has a loving family, a growing medical support staff, increasing funding from Mark Gerson and others, and, above all, a presence to oversee all and provide miracle after miracle, none more striking than with Rita or Kuku. "God fills in the gaps," Catena says.

CHAPTER 5

The Pharmacist
and the Baby

IN MARCH 2021, HELEN WOLDAY, a thirty-seven-year-old pharmacist at Allina Health System Hospital in Minneapolis, has a dream.

The dream is so vivid that she can't let it go. Helen is originally from Ethiopia, and in the dream, a baby less than a year old is given to her by a familiar woman. It seems to Helen there is a message that she needs to figure out. In the dream, the baby has a heart problem and needs surgery. She is told that she is the only one who can save the baby.

She recognizes the woman who hands her the baby. It is the famous Ethiopian actress Meseret Mebrate.

"You know, this is not just a regular dream I have every day," Helen tells me in an interview. "In fact, I don't remember most of my dreams, and none of them are in any way life-changing. This dream comes to me completely out of the blue. There is a woman in Ethiopia. She's an artist, a famous actress. She's the one who brings me the baby; I don't know in my dream if it is a boy or a girl. She tells me this baby has a heart problem and needs open-heart surgery, and the baby is dying.

"Then she hands the baby to me," Helen continues, "and she says, 'You're the only one who can help and save this baby.' I can see that the baby is in a lot of discomfort, and I am very sad. I say, 'Well, I am a pharmacist. I'm not a doctor, not a heart surgeon. So there's no way I can do this.' She says, 'No, you're the only one who can help this child.'

"During the dream, I take the sick baby from Meseret. I then turn around and see a hospital bed, and doctors are working on the baby, doing open-heart surgery. When they complete the surgery, the baby is awake, and the doctors say the baby is better. I pick the baby up again and Meseret is there and says, 'You saved the baby.' I say 'No, the doctors saved the baby.' She says without me the baby would not have made it. I continue to hold the baby in my arms as I wake up from the dream."

Helen's mother is very religious. When Helen tells her about the dream, she immediately says that Helen has to start looking for Meseret. Helen says she doesn't know how to find her, but her mother tells her this vision needs to be acted on right away. Helen, meanwhile, is so upset by the dream that she's unable to work her usual job running COVID clinics in Minneapolis and giving COVID vaccines.

She decides to take time off until she figures out what to do.

Helen hasn't been to Ethiopia for twenty years, and she

doesn't have many connections there anymore. But it turns out her brother's friend used to work with Meseret, and is a friend of hers.

"So my brother connects me with his friend, and I call her the very next day and I say I had a very vivid dream. And I cannot let it go. I need you to help me find Meseret." The friend agrees to help and messages Meseret on Instagram.

Meseret responds, telling her friend to give Helen her phone number.

Helen calls Meseret and says, "I know this is going to sound very odd, but I want you to know that I had a dream about you handing me a baby with a heart condition, and you told me to help the baby. This has been bothering me ever since I had the dream. If you know anything, can you help me?"

Meseret is crying. "You would not believe what has happened here over the last few days," she tells Helen. As it turns out, Meseret is like a surgery ambassador, a fundraiser who arranges for Ethiopian kids with heart disease to get their treatment either abroad or inside the country. She says she just went to one fundraising event for Making the Grade: Hope for African Youth, an organization that helps Ethiopian youths with education, housing, nourishment, and health services.

At the event, a woman asked Meseret to see a baby with a heart condition. When she went to the room, there was a mom sitting and weeping.

The mother told Meseret that her baby had Down syndrome and heart disease, and said she believed the baby had a hole in her heart. The baby was seven months old and looked very ill to Meseret. The mother's name was Mary, and the baby was named Chrstuyan. The doctors in Ethiopia said that they couldn't do the procedure there and that she didn't have a lot of time left. Meanwhile, Chrstuyan was crying nonstop and couldn't be breastfed. In Ethiopia there is no word for Down syndrome, and unfortunately the condition is often treated with neglect and shame and stigma, as children are hidden and parents are wrongly blamed, as though the condition is a form of retribution from the gods.

Heart disease is far different in Ethiopia than in the US. In Ethiopia, there is still a lot of rheumatic heart disease, a consequence of untreated strep throat, which can cause severe damage to heart valves. There are also many cases of uncorrected congenital heart disease, since many Ethiopians born with imperfect hearts like Chrstuyan cannot get surgery. About 50 percent of Down syndrome babies are born with heart disease, and most often the problem is an atrioventricular septal defect, commonly referred to as a "hole in the heart." Meseret tells Helen she feels helpless and doesn't know what to do. She sends Helen a photo of beautiful, smiling Chrstuyan, and Helen immediately knows: "I need to help her." She asks Meseret to connect them.

Making the Grade has started the fundraising, and some people help the family start a GoFundMe account. They are able to raise about $3,500 for Chrstuyan, but she needs about $10,000 to go out of the country to have the heart procedure done, so they are still short about $6,500. And they don't know which hospital or which country to go to for the procedure.

Mary feels that attempts to fundraise for her baby daughter are going to take too long, longer than the baby actually has left. When Helen calls Mary from Minnesota, at first Mary doesn't think Helen can help and doesn't stay on the phone with her. She thinks she's just another well-meaning empty do-gooder. But Helen doesn't let it go. "I call her back the next day, and I say, 'I had a dream about a baby.' I tell her the whole story so now she doesn't think I'm just some crazy woman calling her from Minnesota trying to convince her her baby is going to be fine." Helen also tells Mary, "I would like to do my part; if this is what I'm called to do by God, I would like to see if the baby is going to be all right."

Mary cries. She says, "God actually sent me an angel."

Helen doesn't raise any more money for Mary, though; she gives her own money. She donates through Making the Grade, and now Mary and Chrstuyan are ready to go, assuming they can find a surgeon to do the operation.

Meanwhile, Dr. Obsinet Merid, a practicing internist in Atlanta, Georgia, and the president of Making the Grade, contacts the legendary missionary and internist Dr. Rick Hodes, who has worked out of Mother Teresa's clinic in Ethiopia, diagnosing severe spinal deformities and congenital heart problems and getting them repaired.

Dr. Hodes has been practicing medicine in Ethiopia for thirty-six years. He tells me in an interview that he believes miracles are much more visible in remote regions of the world like Ethiopia. Like Mother Teresa, he cares for those in need, with a single-minded focus on saving lives, one person at a time. He shares a thought from the Talmud Sanhedrin scripture: "Whoever saves one life saves the world entire."

He connects impoverished patients with state-of-the-art surgeries, and his work is legendary. He arranges for children with severe spinal deformities to receive corrective surgery so they can walk straight again. Mary and her son Chrstuyan are coming to the right place. Dr. Hodes says to me, "A medical miracle is something that goes beyond good medical care, where you need the intervention of divine timing or something that science doesn't explain."

Hodes says that Chrstuyan is not likely to survive much longer because of the hole in her heart. So he arranges for a surgery for her in India as fast as possible. Hodes says they operate on babies with Down syndrome there. Hodes calls Down's babies "angels in disguise."

Mary brings Chrstuyan to India and talks with Helen on the phone twice a day for guidance, support, and faith. Mary says that Helen's dream brings her hope. The day of the surgery, they are both in tears as they FaceTime each other from India and Minneapolis. Helen knows she is participating in a miracle.

The surgery to repair the atrioventricular septal defect is performed at the AIMS Amrita Hospital in Kochi, southwest India. Baby Chrstuyan amazes her doctors by surviving the surgery and doing well. These are the doctors in Helen's dream. They are highly skilled and willing to operate on a baby this young, including one with Down syndrome.

After the surgery, Helen keeps in close touch with Mary

and Chrstuyan, who will soon be four years old. "We are like family now," Helen says. "I talk to Mary about three times a week. She's become a second family to me."

Helen wonders if she will have more disturbing dreams. Then, one night, she dreams she is going down a hill, slips, and ends up in a peat hole.

"And then big rocks start falling on me, and my whole body gets buried up to my neck, and then a rock hits my head. I know I am about to die and I am screaming, but nobody can help me. And then I see an angel giving me a hand. I say, 'I can't push the rocks off me. They're too heavy.' The angel says that 'I can.' And then I push the rocks off and he holds my hand and pulls me out."

When Helen wakes up, she remembers that last rock hitting her in the head, and in fact she has been having headaches. She goes to the doctor to order an MRI, and they find a brain tumor. At first they think it is malignant, before later changing their minds. "The Mayo Clinic doctors tell me I probably have two months or a year to live, that the tumor looks like a glioma. But now they think it is a benign tumor. It hasn't grown at all."

Helen knows her dreams are divine messages and the angel is there in the dream to save her and show that she will live on.

In September 2024, Helen travels to Ethiopia to meet Mary and young Chrstuyan for the first time. She eagerly anticipates the trip, and knows that this relationship is no coincidence. "I truly believe that God puts specific people in our lives that need help and also he gives us the resources to complete the task. I feel so blessed to be a part of baby Chrstuyan's journey. It's all God's plan." When Helen finally arrives at Mary's house, there is a huge feast awaiting her. A large plate of tibs (beef fried in butter with onion and garlic), doro wot (chicken with berbere sauce, butter, onions, chili, cardamom, and a hard-boiled egg), kitfo (raw beef seasoned with chili), and injera (a sourdough flatbread). A large plate of popcorn, coffee, and a delicious Ethiopian honey tart and several other desserts follow. The coffee is the best Helen has ever had, its earthen taste mixed with fruit and spice.

Helen says this is one of the happiest days of her life, to see the outcome of her dream in the flesh. A happy family preserved. "I got to meet baby Chrstuyan and her family. Her family welcomed me with lots of love, tears in their eyes, and a big feast. What a wonderful family! Chrstuyan is doing so well. She is so beautiful, funny, and so loving. She has two sisters and one brother. They all love and care for her. I am witnessing the goodness of God!"

Children with Down syndrome are frequently misunderstood and mistreated, not just in Ethiopia but around the world. Many may have attention problems, or social withdrawal, but not Chrstuyan. Not a shred of it. She is fun-loving, social, highly interactive, engaging at all times. Her family says she does not have temper tantrums and is not impulsive. Some children with Down syndrome have strong social skills, and Chrstuyan is clearly one of them.

Helen is right. Her dream was a message about the preciousness of a single life. A message from God about how to cherish Chrstuyan and save her, one of His prize creations.

CHAPTER 6

Team 43

CORPORAL DAVE SMITH IS A Marine Corps infantryman stationed in Iraq in 2004. When he finishes his time in the military in 2007, he struggles to acclimate to a new civilian life. The transition is very hard. "My friends are still going to war, and I'm sitting here in college. . . . To be in war and to fight and kill other people and then try to put it behind you has a long-term effect," he says to me in an interview for this book. From 2009 to 2013, he attends college, starting at El Camino College in Los Angeles and then later transferring up to UC Berkeley. At both schools he is surrounded by college students who have different life experiences. "I am quite frustrated. I am out of place and quite angry. I don't think the other students know how to view me. I don't know how to interact with them." There are also people who are against anything that he has done because it is connected with the military or George Bush, and Dave is targeted with guilt by association.

But events in LA in 2010 and at Berkeley in early 2012,

when Smith's depression gets a lot worse, really shape the miracle that occurs one night.

He is in Los Angeles in 2010 and doesn't know where to find help. He meets Clay, who had also been an infantry Marine. Clay had been shot and wounded. He had lost friends in the war. But he has been going to counseling, and that makes Dave feel comfortable doing the same. Clay also introduces Dave to mountain biking, which helps relieve stress. "Biking is what allows me to get outside of my own head and not constantly think about war and all of the other stresses of everyday life," Dave says. "When I'm out on a bike trail pushing my limits and processing the terrain and enjoying nature and making split-second decisions, there is no time for other thoughts. It's an endorphin rush, it's exercise, and it has allowed me to find peace, even if only for a few hours at a time." Soon Dave is doing much better.

And yet, only a year later, Clay commits suicide. Dave is devastated. "I vow to continue with counseling and not give it up. But then almost a year after he took his life, I am at Berkeley and am falling apart. And one night I drink every bottle of alcohol in my apartment and then I put a loaded shotgun in my mouth. The alcohol plays a role in getting me to that point with the gun, and it has me completely disinhibited and ready to go, but then somehow, I don't pull the trigger."

"What stops you?" I ask. "The vast majority in that situation don't stop."

"I don't really know," Dave says. "To this day, it's hard to believe. I am drunk, I don't think I can stop myself, but then all of a sudden, I think of my friend Clay. I feel him there in the room with me, his actual presence, like his ghost, trying to hold me back. I know what all of his friends and family went through after he killed himself. And I picture my family and I don't want to do that to anyone myself. I want to hit the reset button. I want a new start. It is Clay's spirit there telling me to hold back. That's what stops me."

Dave Smith tells me with great sadness that he is sure Clay had been sent to him as a messenger from God to warn him, to set him on the right path, to teach him to mountain bike as a way of coping even if it wasn't enough to save himself. Clay, already sensing he would not make it, was giving Dave a chance to live. And then, the following year, the vision of Clay pulls Dave back from the brink. He has no other explanation for surviving in that moment.

"How close do you come to pulling that trigger?" I ask.

"I have loaded the shotgun and as soon as I put it here"—he gestures toward his face—"I have a very, very, very strong reaction. You know this is not what is supposed to be for me. This is not God's plan for my life."

Smith says he feels an almost physical force pushing the gun away from his face, the ghostly hand of Clay. At the same time, the image comes into his head of mountain biking, another gift from Clay.

Dave says that substance abuse played a big role in Clay ending his life. "I believe that had he made it through that night he'd still be with us today. There's a lot of people who consume substances and it puts them in a hard place. And the next thing you know, they decide to put a very permanent solution in place for what is really a short-term problem." Dave is one of the rare exceptions. "Clay's presence is there to keep me from pulling the trigger in the last second. I think about how much Clay had to offer the world if he had just stayed with us. And thinking that, it is no longer possible for me to pull the trigger anymore."

Just a few days after his near suicide, Dave gets an unexpected call from the Bush Center about the W100K mountain-bike ride. "The Bush people call me to come because they hear I ride bikes," Dave says. "Without Clay, that call would never have come. He told me that mountain biking will give me something to live for. The call comes right after my attempt. A literal lifeline from God." Smith goes on to become a spokesperson for the launch of the Bush Institute's important initiative on the "invisible wounds of war."

❧

THE EVENT THAT first set Corporal Smith on his downward spiral occurred during combat in Iraq back in 2004, when he became trapped on the roof of a burning building with the other members of his platoon one night, holding a rifle without a light on its end. He saw a group of blurry targets in the night moving toward their position, and he fired without making proper identification.

He wounded a fellow Marine, a close friend. This cost his friend part of his foot, which was amputated. "I am nineteen years old when it happens," Smith tells me. "And this is really difficult for me. I don't know if I have just ruined this man's life, or if he is drinking himself to death, or what happens."

By 2024, Dave and his Norwegian wife, Katrina, have three babies, with a fourth on the way, and Dave finally reveals to me the full details of the night in 2004 when he wounds a friend, leading to the haunted years that follow.

"I was raised in a Christian home," he says, "where I was taught not to hurt others." Yet from a very young age, Dave was always interested in the military, and he joined the Marine Corps when he graduated from high school. By then, the war in Iraq was in full motion.

"My first deployment to Iraq is in 2004. We experience a lot of fighting. We fight through a city called Najaf. And a place in the Gulf called the Wadi al-Salam Cemetery, which is filled with massive holy sites. One night—I think it is August seventeenth or eighteenth—we get a call that there is an Iraqi police station which has been taken over by a militia."

The militia has already murdered all of the police officers and is now wearing their uniforms. They are pulling over local civilians and assaulting and murdering them. So Dave's group is tasked with stopping them.

"It is going to be a nighttime mission. We load up in armored vehicles, which we only do when it's going to be a really fierce night. When we get close, a couple of miles outside the city, we start taking a lot of gunfire, rockets, even IEDs. The city that we are going into is a place called Kufa, with no US troop presence in it. So we know we are in for a tough fight."

On this night, Dave has not mounted a night-vision optic to his weapon. It's a heavy machine gun called a SAW, or a squad automatic weapon. It's quite heavy, and when a soldier has a night-vision optic mounted on the top, it's very difficult to use. The optic is made for engaging targets at a long range, usually from a lying-down position where the weapon is stable. But Dave and his team are going inside buildings. For these reasons, he does not think the night vision makes sense, but he says, "I have wondered every single day since whether I wasn't being sloppy or unfocused without sufficient regard to my comrades' well-being."

Dave and his comrades secure a building, and then things happen very quickly. "We're under attack, and people are trying to reach into the building to get towards us, or are dropping grenades down off the side of the building to keep people from getting in. It is very intense. And in this chaos and confusion, I see a group of targets that move down an alleyway towards our position. And without night vision I can't see clearly. I fire into that group of targets, and I wound a Marine because I don't realize that they are Marines."

The Marine Dave hits is a close friend of his, and he is sent home and has part of his foot amputated.

"I have always wanted to be in the military," Dave says again, his voice wavering with emotion. "I have always wanted to be a very good soldier. What happens that night is an unforgivable sin because it is within my control. There are a lot of things that happen within war that you can't control, but something like this I can.

"If I mount my night vision as soon as we go up to the

rooftop, then I keep one of my close friends from getting wounded—by me. Knowing I can and don't prevent this is very hard. I feel the other guys look down on me after this. I know that this is in my mind, but still I feel very alienated. I hide. I am ashamed. I feel like an outcast and this is very hard on a base with less than one hundred guys altogether. I feel I can't get over what's happened."

I pause. I can feel the emotion even across Zoom all these years later from Norway. "What happens after that, Dave?" I ask gently. "You are still serving?"

"We are in the very beginning of a deployment, so I am deployed for another seven months after that. I question myself a lot. I hesitate. How do I make sure that I don't do this again? At the same time, how do I make sure that I continue to raise my weapon, to engage targets, to protect my team? I am terrified of ever making that mistake again.

"I was an eighteen-year-old kid from Akron, Ohio, just out of high school. And then the next thing I know I'm a United States Marine in a foreign country, kicking down doors, knowing that there's somebody with a gun on the other side of them, knowing that there are people on the other side of that door who are trying to kill me. And at the same time there are innocent people too. So when you take a door, it's not like you can just go in and spray bullets and be like, Oh, everyone's bad. So you have to make a lot of very difficult decisions in a very compressed time frame. Under maximum chaos.

"The Marine Corps is an identity to me. The people that I am deployed with, we are family. I mean, I would take a bullet for any of those guys still today. Love them. And when you leave the military, you kind of lose your tribe. You lose your group of people, your connections. When I leave the military, I feel I don't have my life's calling anymore. What am I going to do next?"

AFTER HE LEAVES the military, Smith can't stop thinking about the error he's made. It haunts him for years afterward. He becomes numb from it and soon develops a drinking problem. The worse he feels, the more he drinks.

He is honorably discharged in 2007, and enrolls first at the community college in Los Angeles in 2008 before later transferring to the University of California, Berkeley, where he scores straight A's but continues to struggle with self-doubt, depression, and alcoholism.

But then comes what Dave eventually will believe is a direct messenger from God.

While in LA, David meets a fellow veteran named Clay, who befriends him and encourages him to take up mountain biking, to seek professional counseling, and to work as a volunteer in veterans' organizations. Clay helps David become less reclusive and more religious, transmitting lifesaving skills to his friend.

"Clay comes into my life completely out of the blue when I have almost no close friends around me," Dave tells me. "Clay is an angel to me."

Clay takes Dave under his wing and talks openly with

him about war and losing friends—things that Dave never had the openness or courage to discuss with anyone before. Clay introduces Dave to veterans' groups, gets him involved with disaster response (Dave finds that helping others is a very healing experience), and introduces him to a massive new circle of friends. "Probably ninety percent of the close friends I have today are as a result of Clay," Dave says. "We bike together and just talk, and somewhere in that process, I begin to find real healing."

Clay is also the first person Dave ever mentions the friendly fire incident to. Until then it was a big secret for Dave, and a source of shame. "But after I share it with Clay, then it isn't really a secret anymore and it is then that I start to find the road to healing." Clay tells Dave that he's speaking to a counselor at the US Department of Veterans Affairs, and invites him to do the same. Dave agrees. "It turns out I need that permission from someone I respect and admire in order to feel like it is okay for me to seek treatment. I overcome the stigma and get started. And over the course of time, things start to get much better for me."

Then, Clay moves away. And one night, Dave receives horrible news: Clay has taken his own life.

"Clay comes into my life suddenly, we become best friends for a short period of time, he changes the trajectory of my life for the better, and then is gone as quick as he comes. The only sense that I can make out of it is that Clay is some sort of an angel or messenger that God sends to me."

SUICIDE AND ATTEMPTED suicide are becoming epidemic among our veterans, especially tragic when you consider that these men and women suffer from depression, anxiety, and post-traumatic stress disorder (PTSD) as a direct result of their efforts defending the United States.

Severe depression is an affliction that often doesn't go away. And it frequently affects people in the prime of life, with members of our military being particularly susceptible to its chokehold. Suicide is among the top nine leading causes of death for people ages ten to sixty-five in the US. Among veterans, there is an average of 17.2 suicide deaths every day in America. According to a Boston University study, around 30,177 post-9/11 war veterans—more than four times those who were killed in the war—died by suicide between 2001 and 2021. Of course, as Dr. Charles Marmar, chief of psychiatry and top PTSD expert, has pointed out to me, even if one in five combat veterans suffer from PTSD, that means that four in five manage to avoid it. Still, if you are one of the 20 percent, it is a war wound that never completely leaves you.

People who die by suicide with a firearm are much less likely to have sought treatment beforehand. The vast majority of suicide attempts by firearms are lethal, and very few who reach the point of a gun in their hand with suicidal intention "walk it back." Dave is one of the very few. Eight out of ten firearm-related deaths are from suicide.

When it comes to veterans with post-traumatic stress disorder, there are many who don't have the full disorder but still suffer from some degree of post-traumatic stress, which interferes with their daily lives. Symptoms include flashbacks, nightmares, anxiety, and the inability to function. The Bush Institute's Military Service Initiative has focused on the "invisible wounds of war" (traumatic brain injury and post-traumatic stress) for more than a decade, in part because of the inspiring story of Marine Corporal David Smith.

Many with PTSD also struggle with substance abuse, including alcoholism, and 85 percent of users relapse and return to drug or alcohol use within one year of treatment. This makes Dave Smith's story and his recovery all the more unlikely.

THE YEAR AFTER Clay's death, and a month after his own near suicide, Dave barely makes it to the long, healing arms of the Bush Center's yearly Warrior 100-kilometer mountain-bike ride, where veterans (and their supporters, including active military) come together from all over the US for an endurance exercise event with their former commander in chief. I have reported on this extraordinary event for over a decade, and Dave is one of its most important participants and a measure of the endeavor's success.

In April 2012, President George W. Bush invites me to the second annual Warrior 100K ride, taking place this year in Amarillo, Texas, at Palo Duro Canyon State Park. Palo Duro features some of the toughest mountain-bike trails in the country. Bush has heard that I am a longtime cyclist who has ridden across the United States, and he issues me a challenge: If I manage to finish the course and promise to focus an interview on fitness and veterans' health, he will give me that exclusive interview for Fox News.

I train for months on my road bike, but nothing prepares me for the conditions that late April in Palo Duro Canyon. It is dry, dusty, and 105 degrees. I cover myself in sunscreen and suck in water from the pouch on my back, called an Osprey. There are also "oasis" pit stops with fruit and Gatorade. But the ride is fierce. I fall many times on the dusty and windy single-track trails, and even ride over a rattlesnake. By the end of the ride, there are cactus needles protruding from my butt.

Still, I manage to finish the course—the first day is seventeen miles of torturous terrain on single-track trails. The three-day ride is a total of one hundred kilometers.

There are nineteen wounded vets and fifty support staff on the ride, along with former First Lady Laura Bush, the Bush staff, and my camera crew. This support group trails us along the road on motorized Gators. I witness how the military works, how they ride in formation, how they call for help when one of them falls, and how they stop to help each other up. I am invigorated and honored to be with them. I stay with Dave Smith for part of the ride. We ride up behind the former president and are proud to be able to keep up with him—at least for a while. He tells his vintage jokes to keep us loose and we marvel at how funny and humble he is. I recall Dave's optimism, and how he rides through the heat without pausing. It is the first time I am meeting him, but I can tell that he has experienced much worse than this heat.

Dave is one of the first to help others up from the ground

when they fall, and he helps me up several times. It is hot and we focus on staying on our bikes and not sliding out when the track suddenly turns dusty or tortuous. Dave seems undeterred by the harsh elements of the day's ride. I do not yet know how close to death he has come.

Afterward, President Bush calls for me. We stand together outside the clubhouse where the veterans are gathering. "What matters to me most is toughness, never giving up," he says. "And you showed me that today in spades. I had very low expectations and you exceeded them by far. You are tough." I am honored to hear this. I know in my heart that never giving up is a path to a miracle. Dave knows it too.

After the first day of riding, there is a dinner in Amarillo that night for the wounded war fighters and their supporters. We all drink a lot of water to compensate for what we have lost during the day. There is a brass band, and the food is fresh and local. Dave Smith is the featured speaker, and I recognize him from the ride.

We all listen closely as Dave tells us that, just a month before this ride, exactly a year since Clay's suicide, he "drinks all the alcohol [he] can find" and brings a shotgun up to his face.

Everyone in the audience is holding their breath, including his mother, who hasn't heard about any of it before. Dave tells us that he doesn't take his life that night, but he is on the edge. Then, a few days later, he receives an invitation to this wounded veterans' mountain-bike ride, an invitation that fills him with hope and keeps him going. And now, bonding with his fellow riders will help him reach the next step. President Bush rushes onto the stage and his hug brings tears to all of us, and Smith says he feels really lucky to be here. We all feel lucky to be here with him.

✤

I RECONNECT WITH Dave in 2017, before the "alumni ride" commemorating a new Veteran Wellness Alliance at the George W. Bush Presidential Center. This year, the ride is connected with the publication of Bush's book *Portraits of Courage*, which features many of these same war fighters, including Dave Smith. I speak with him in the Bush Library on the Southern Methodist University campus under the beautiful life-size painting Bush has done of him, and then I interview him again on camera in the early morning in front of the Prairie Chapel School, just in front of Bush's ranch in Crawford, Texas. He is doing better than ever, having just married the love of his life, Katrina. He has also moved to Norway, working as a marketing manager in a startup business.

We ride together over some of the challenging terrain on the ranch, sections aptly named "twister" and "waterfall." Dave also rides with Robert Young, who was his troop leader in Iraq and helped him get through the friendly-fire incident. Dave spends time with Peter Way, a double amputee who rides a hand cycle. When Way's cycle hits a rock on a steep uphill the wrong way and he falls and injures his shoulder, it is Dave who breaks away from the ride to bring Way to the hospital.

In an interview after the ride, President Bush comments

to me about Dave and the painting he did of him, which shows the haunted expression that characterized him so well before the suicide attempt in 2012. "Smith is strong. The fact that he comes here means a lot. He was really hurt emotionally. At one time he was suicidal and thankfully he walked it back and has got his life back together. A lot of it has to do with serving other people. It helped him get his spirit back. Now he's married. Doing great.

"Smith is a great example of how to recover," the former president says with strong conviction. "Vets have been hurt. Vets helping vets is the best way to transition from the military to civilian life. It's peer-to-peer counseling. It works—it is a three-step process. The first step is to admit you have a problem. Pretty logical. If a vet keeps it inside, no one will understand what he thinks, no one can possibly relate to what he feels like. If he or she doesn't share, obviously that leads to negative consequences. Secondly, when you seek help, you and I can be sympathetic, but we can't possibly relate to what it's like to see a friend killed in combat. And yet, there are others who can. And here in this group, people have progressed from severe depression, from a severe case of post-traumatic stress, or a more moderate case, or in some cases a light case of it, and they can share with their pal what it took to come back. And so it's logical. And it works. Thirdly, transitioning back to civilian life involves transitioning to more positive feelings— how can I make a meaningful contribution as a civilian?"

During that 2017 ride, Dave talks to me about how post-traumatic growth has helped him. The haunted expression that President Bush painted in his eyes is now gone. "After the traumatic experience I went through, in order to survive I had to learn to be more affectionate in relationships, closer to God, never giving up."

علم

WHEN I CONNECT with Dave again in 2024, calling him on Zoom, it's been twenty years since the friendly-fire incident in Iraq, and twelve years after the events that finally saved him. I haven't seen him since the 2017 event at the Bush Library and the accompanying alumni ride, but he has kept in close touch with the other riders and with the Bush Institute, building and sharing strength and stories and helping each other up when they stumble.

The war fighters and their former commander in chief are known as Team 43, and they play a crucial role in Smith's recovery beginning with his first W100K bike ride in 2012.

"It fills gaps. I am hurting, I have made the decision that I am not going to kill myself, but my heart feels like it is literally breaking into pieces every single day for months and months after that. But while I am down there on the ride, I am around other guys who have similar backgrounds, who've been in the military, been injured, lost friends. And I make some really significant lifelong friends there, and I feel safe again. And I make the decision that if I ever feel like doing something like this again, I am actually just going to pick up the phone and call Colonel Miguel Howe [then head of the Bush Military Institute] and just sleep underneath someone's desk at the Bush Center for a couple days to keep myself safe.

"The first time you meet President Bush, it's very surreal. I never thought I would meet a president. And then he's very casual and he's polite, and he shakes your hand and says hi. And he looks you in the eyes and he tells you, you know, thank you for your service. But after I tell that story at the dinner, he comes up and gives me a big hug. I remember looking at him and seeing that he has tears running down his face. It is a deep interaction."

Being with Team 43 on that mountain-bike ride in 2012 begins Smith on the road to healing.

Faith becomes very important to him again, after losing touch with it in Iraq. "I had numbed myself entirely to the point where I didn't feel anything. I didn't want to feel anything. But after that incident, I learn to feel again. I reconnect with God. I didn't know what to do with all that emotional pain that I had inside. But the Bush Center, Team Rubicon, the VA, they help me to get back on track."

Smith says that God guides his recovery. After the near suicide, and after the bike ride, he finishes college at Berkeley and then signs up for a yearlong Christian missionary trip around the world. "I travel to eleven countries in eleven months and do all kinds of aid and development projects. Work in orphanages." Every day he has one simple prayer: "God, I am so sorry. Please help me to be a good man." Smith says that this prayer leads to his becoming the best version of himself he can be.

Smith says that he has never been happier. He loves his life, his wife, and his family. As he looks back on his miracle recovery, he gives thanks to Clay for teaching him the first steps and the spirit of Clay for getting him to the Bush bike trail, where his recovery could continue.

CHAPTER 7

The Rebbe

IT IS A SUNDAY AFTERNOON in 1989, and the renowned Rebbe, Rabbi Menachem Schneerson, is seated in a small room near his office in Crown Heights, Brooklyn. He is receiving his congregants, as well as others (Jews and non-Jews) who are not his congregants, for his famous "dollars." Hundreds of men, women, and children pass by to receive his blessings and a dollar for them to give to tzedakah (charity).

Among those standing in line are Nathan Litkowski and most of his family. Nathan had been the Rebbe's carpenter a decade before. The Rebbe gives a dollar to his two boys who are present.

"Then he gives one to me," says Nathan, "but he is holding that dollar, and he will not let go of the dollar. And I am afraid to look in his sharp blue eyes."

The Rebbe says to Nathan in Yiddish, "Yau bistu," which means, "Where are you?"

"I'm here," a shocked Nathan tells the Rebbe.

The Rebbe replies, "Why are you not coming to me?"

Nathan understands the Rebbe is asking why he doesn't come regularly. "I'm always dirty," he answers. "My hands are so dirty. I walk around with a T-shirt; I do construction, as you know. I am embarrassed to go with dirty clothing with no time for a suit, no nothing."

"You come the way you are," the Rebbe says. "You don't have to impress me. I know you."

The great Rebbe gives his former carpenter a blessing for each of his boys and one for their father, but Nathan knows he senses something is wrong, which is why he was holding onto the dollar. The Rebbe says a special blessing for Nathan's third child, who has just been born, named Israel. The Rebbe notices that though Nathan's two oldest sons are there with him, Israel is not present.

Nathan can't look the great man in the eyes.

ﯨ

NATHAN, THE REBBE'S former carpenter, was born in a little city in Ukraine, about one hundred miles from Warsaw, Poland. After some time living in Uzbekistan his family got a visa to come to Israel in 1969, when he was nine years old. In the early 1970s, Nathan and his mother moved to Crown Heights. His father had survived a pogrom in which most of his family was killed, but then had died when Nathan was very young.

"I first met the Rebbe a couple of weeks before my bar mitzvah in 1973," says Nathan. "He had unbelievable blue eyes and the most gorgeous smile. And if you looked for a split second in his eyes, it was like a light shining in your soul."

Nathan began working for the Rebbe in 1979. The Rebbe created a great opportunity for Nathan at a time when he was completely lost. Because he was dyslexic and nobody knew it, he had always sat in the back of the class at school, where he memorized how to pray. He was doing poorly at studies because of his dyslexia but still had managed to learn his prayers. When he was seventeen, he left Orthodox Jewish school to start making money because his mother was very poor.

One of the Rebbe's assistants asked him then, in a moment that changed his life, "What do you like to do?"

"I like to do carpentry," he said. "I have good hands and I can make shelving, bookcases. I do mahogany doors. I'll do anything you want. I used to fix locks, doors, hinges, whatever you want."

Nathan was given the honor of renovating the Rebbe's entire office. He worked there for a year and a half. Every morning, the Rebbe would say, "Make sure you make the prayer." Even though the Rebbe was an extremely busy man, he would check in on Nathan. After one particularly full day, the Rebbe asked, "Did you eat?" This shocked Nathan. "I shake my head, yes, I ate, I ate, and I feel the love that the Rebbe keeps for me."

It was while Nathan was working in the Rebbe's office in 1980 that he met his wife, Chaya. "I am installing a big Andersen window for the Rebbe's office," Nathan recalls. "And, at that time, I feel pretty good. I'm making twenty dollars a day. Everybody knows me. You know, this is the young boy working for the Rebbe. It makes me more popular. And then from the Rebbe's window, I see a beautiful woman walking to a house three houses away. The family Malamet house. Very wealthy. He is a printer, prints stamps for different countries. She goes there to babysit. And around four or five every day she passes by, and I look at her."

A friend who works with Nathan tells him to stop looking at the girl. "What's wrong with you? You're in the Rebbe's holiest place."

"Maybe this is what the Rebbe wants to happen," Nathan replies. "Maybe he is like a father making a shidduch [match]. My own father died so long ago, and the Rebbe knows that and stands in his place."

Three weeks later, Nathan and Chaya are engaged, and now they have been married for forty-three years.

علم

THE CHABAD-LUBAVITCH IS a Hasidic Jewish movement founded by Rabbi Schneur Zalman of Liadi, in 1772 in Russia. In 1951, Rabbi Menachem Mendel Schneerson, the Rebbe, officially became the seventh leader of this movement. With millions of followers during his life and since, Schneerson is known to have been more responsible for the spiritual awakening of world Jewry than any other leader in recent times. He was born in 1902 in Nikolaev, Russia, to the erudite and kind Rebbetzin Chana Schneerson and the renowned scholar and leader Rabbi Levi Yitzchak.

When Menachem Mendel was nine years old, he courageously dove into the Black Sea and saved the life of a little boy who had lost control of a small rowboat. This need to save others in danger came to characterize his later years, and by the time he was a teen, he was deeply immersed in the study of Torah. In 1928 he married the sixth Rebbe's daughter, Rebbetzin Chaya Mushka. They would go on to be married for sixty years. While still in Europe, the future seventh Rebbe studied math and science at the University of Berlin and at the Sorbonne in Paris. But then some of the family, including Menachem Mendel, escaped from the Nazis in occupied France in 1941 and found safe haven in New York.

In 1951, Rabbi Menachem Mendel Schneerson assumed the leadership of the Chabad movement from his father-in-law. For the next twenty-five years he received his followers in private audiences three times a week, from just before nightfall to long into the night, several hundred visitors each time. He received not just Hasidic Jews but men and women from all walks of life. Some nights, the last of the visitors would depart well after daybreak. He had learned from his father-in-law that "when two people meet, something good should result for a third." And the new Rebbe did his best to extend his focus, advice, and blessings for all he met. Eventually, the requests for meetings with the Rebbe grew to such a point that he was no longer able to accommodate all of them. He took to written correspondence, reading and responding to several sacks of mail each day.

In 1986, the Rebbe began conducting a weekly receiving line. Each Sunday, the Rebbe would stand in a small room near his office as thousands of men, women, and children filed past to see him and receive his blessing. Many used the opportunity to pose a question and obtain a word of advice. To each of them the Rebbe gave a dollar bill, appointing them as his personal agent to give it to the charity of their choice, in this way extending a "mitzvah" to benefit others. He famously said, "Every soul is a diamond. Can one grow tired of counting diamonds?" He became known as a miracle worker because hundreds of incredible stories sprang from his daily interactions with his disciples. Once, when asked if he performed supernatural acts, he answered, "The ability to work miracles is not confined to a select group of individuals, but is within reach of each and every one of us. We each possess a soul that is a spark of Godliness. So we each have the power to transcend the limitations imposed upon us by our physical natures, no matter how formidable they may seem."

۶طۿ

THERE ARE COUNTLESS stories of the Rebbe's participation in medical miracles, but none more striking than the one involving Nathan and Chaya Litkowski's son Israel.

When Israel is born in 1989, he is sweating all the time and he just doesn't gain weight. He also seems lethargic. So Nathan and Chaya take him to a local doctor, who tells them not to worry. He assures them that Israel will grow out of it, and that they just need to wait and see.

"But he looks like a little bird, literally," says Nathan. "He is eating very few bottles of milk. You can see the skin and bones. You see more of the bones. It is very, very scary."

So Nathan and Chaya, who at the time lived a block away from the Rebbe, write a note to the Rebbe to ask him for a prayer. He replies by saying to check the mezuzah—a piece of parchment inscribed with a scripture, kept in a case that hangs from a doorpost—on Israel's door. The mezuzah has lines inside from the Shema prayer, and when Nathan checks it, he finds that the letter Mem (in the shape of a circle) inside the mezuzah is broken at the bottom, so that now the Mem is in the shape of two circles, like two matching moons.

Nathan tells Rabbi Groner, who works as the Rebbe's secretary, that the mezuzah letter was broken and he has fixed it. But then, a few days later, Rabbi Groner calls him. Nathan goes to the office, and the Rebbe is there and tells him to check Israel's heart.

Nathan is shocked. "Why?" he asks. At first, the Rebbe hesitates. But then he says the Mem is at the center. And the heart is the center of the body, the Rebbe says; the heart pumps and controls everything. "You should go and check his heart," the Rebbe says again. Then Nathan realizes that the Mem is in the shape of a heart, and the bottom of the Mem inside the mezuzah was broken. It was right at the part of the Shema prayer that says, "The Lord is one."

In Jewish teaching, the spiritual and physical are one with each other. If you have a defect on your door in your spiritual (mezuzah), then it has to be linked to the physical. The Rebbe, through Rabbi Groner, suggests that they bring the baby right away to see Dr. Richard Golinko, a pediatric cardiologist at Mount Sinai Hospital in New York. Rabbi Groner arranges for the visit. Golinko finds a problem that had been previously missed: a congenital narrowing of his aortic valve. He passes a balloon through the femoral artery in Israel's groin and tries to open up the valve, but it doesn't work. Now it is clear that the boy is going to need open-heart surgery, but Golinko feels he is too young (only seven months) and should wait until he is bigger, around three years old, when it will be safer if an operation is needed. But there is also a duct coming from the heart that is still open that generally closes on its own within three days of birth (known as a patent ductus arteriosus). This duct connects the pulmonary artery and the aorta, which allows the fetal circulation to bypass the lungs in the womb. The lungs aren't working then, since the fetus is getting all its oxygen from the mother (via the placenta). But once a baby is born, the duct gets in the way and leads to the lungs having to do much more work as fluid starts to build up. It is crucial for this duct to close for a baby to use its lungs properly and have a normal life, but for Israel it hasn't happened.

This duct is another big reason to do the surgery, but Israel is very weak. Nathan worries that young Israel will do poorly and fail to thrive without the operation but also that he will die from the operation.

"We worry we can't do the operation because he will not survive," Nathan says. "He is very skinny. We feel it is a suicidal thing to do to operate when he is like this. So we feel we have to wait. Golinko insists we have to wait." On top of everything else, Nathan and Chaya also don't have compatible blood with Israel, so they need to find the right blood to do it. This particular blood type is rare. Then it turns out the woman whom Chaya was babysitting for when she and Nathan first met has compatible blood, and she volunteers to donate for Israel. "I know this is a sign from God," Nathan says.

When the Rebbe hears about what is happening, he tells Rabbi Groner to get in touch with Nathan with this message: "You've got to do the operation and everything will be fine." This stands in direct contrast with what the doctors are saying. Nathan and Chaya tell the doctors, "Our Rebbe says go ahead and do it." The doctors look at them and say, "Who is this Rebbe? Who is this guy? What are you talking about? We are the doctors."

It takes weeks for Nathan and Chaya to convince them, but the doctors finally give the green light. But even then, there is still a delay. Their insurance coverage is almost canceled but ultimately is not.

"It takes a couple more months to prepare, to get him everything they need for such a delicate operation," says Nathan. "I go to the Rebbe a few times with my oldest sons. The Rebbe gives me a dollar for my oldest son, a dollar for my middle son. I start to walk away and Rabbi Groner stops me and says, 'The Rebbe wants you back.'"

The Rebbe asks Nathan, "How's your little one doing?" Nathan tells him that they have the doctors and everything else is finally in order, and then the Rebbe gives Nathan a dollar for Israel. "He should have everlasting life," he says to Nathan.

Shortly after—right before the operation—Israel has a cardiac arrest and nearly dies.

Chaya recalls these dangerous times: "He gets really sick one night and his pediatrician Dr. Rosen listens to him breathing over the phone and says to go to the hospital right away. We run there. They put him into a room and you see the lights flashing, and they're saying, 'Code blue, code blue.'" As a mother, Chaya can't bear to see them rushing in and out of the room. Israel stops breathing, and after they eventually get him to breathe again, they put him on heart medication. Now the doctors agree with the Rebbe and don't want to wait for the surgery any longer.

The operation takes place when Israel is eight months old. They close the patent ductus and open the aortic valve, and Israel survives. It is "a pure living miracle," Nathan says. "He looks like a little monkey with millions of wires attached. He stays in the hospital for a long time. More than a month."

The doctors are amazed at Israel's recovery. Right after the surgery, he wants to get up and is pulling out all the wires to the monitor. He is still on heart medication, but when they forget to give him one of the medicines, he still does well. "He's doing amazing," one of the doctors tells Nathan.

ﻋﻠﻴﻪ

WHEN ISRAEL IS two years old, his father takes him to see the Rebbe for the first of many visits. Once Israel becomes healthy, the Rebbe gives him dollar bills and looks straight into his eyes each time he sees him. It is clear to Nathan that the Rebbe looks at Israel as someone special. Nathan says the Rebbe becomes more and more attached to Israel.

Thirty-five years after the operation, I speak to Israel, who tells me his whole life has been shaped by this experience. "The Rebbe's impact is beyond time, beyond his own life. And what I mean by that is knowing the fact that in the past, he blessed me and took so much care and so much attention, gave me so much love as a child. Most of the major decisions in my life as a human being and as a person, as a husband, as a father, have been tremendously impacted by the Rebbe's directives in my life. I consider myself a follower first and foremost."

Israel says that he identifies the Rebbe as someone who "is just a man," but with spiritual powers and a direct connection to God. The Rebbe was able to help Israel and others because of that connection. He compares the Rebbe's piercing look with a CT scan looking into your soul. "But how do you prove it scientifically? You can't. We don't have the advanced technology yet to prove that.

"Dr. Golinko was from a nonreligious background. But every time he would see me, he would pull up his sleeve and say, 'Come on, could you put on tefillin with me?' which as you know is a very religious ceremony to do. And I would ask him, 'Why are you doing this?' He would say, 'Because when it comes to you, I saw some amazing miracles. And I see the truth. And I'm inspired.'"

Israel says that Dr. Golinko was one of the best doctors around, at the top of his game, but in the end, even he acknowledged that everything is in God's hands. Golinko's life was changed too by the miracle of Israel's survival. "It's very important to understand that there is no disconnect between religion and spirituality and modern medicine. The Rebbe wanted us to go through modern medicine and through nature at the same time. See a miracle. Be guided by it. The Rebbe saved my life."

Israel's mother, Chaya, says the Rebbe "had the knowledge and vision on lots of things, but until you're in it, you really don't get it. And this was our turn. It was us this time. And yes, miracles happen. Doctors have abilities, but it is only God who knows where things are going."

❧

IN MARCH 1994, Rabbi Schneerson, then ninety-one years old, is admitted to NYU Hospital for Joint Diseases for seizures following a small stroke, having fully recovered from gallbladder surgery two years before. His neurologist is the top seizure specialist in the country, Orrin Devinsky (a matter of public record). Dr. Devinsky says he is optimistic about the Rebbe's chance of recovery. He assigns Ludmilla Bronfin, his top young neurology resident, to take care of Schneerson. Dr. Bronfin says that the Rebbe has already lost his ability to communicate by then, and is incapacitated with a stroke. Still, the requests for miracles pour in. Many call and clamor to come to his bedside for more dollars, but the great Rebbe is too sick to reply and cannot see any visitors.

Despite Dr. Bronfin and Dr. Devinsky's best efforts, he does not improve. The great light from his sharp blue eyes is diminished. He is soon discharged, but a few months later he has another stroke and is admitted to Beth Israel Hospital, where he dies. He lacks the one final miracle he needs to save himself. Dr. Bronfin says it shows we are all human in God's eyes.

But his message and his inspiration will carry on for many generations. Indeed, the great Rebbe's miracles extend beyond the grave, even touching me. A few months after he dies, I am working late on the neurology wards at NYU's Tisch Hospital when I spy a beautiful young resident, her head buried in a patient's chart. She looks tired, but I ask her out for a cup of coffee the next day.

Months later, I am smitten, and she tells me that she was one of the Rebbe's final doctors before he left this world. Dr. Ludmilla "Luda" Bronfin goes on to become my wife and the mother to our three wonderful children. Is our marriage a miracle conceived by God, and channeled through the great Rebbe even after his death? Is this match between me and my wife a miracle similar in timbre to the spiritual match that the Rebbe once conceived for Nathan and Chaya? I believe it is, but I will leave it to you, the reader, to decide.

PART II

Prayers
for the
Soul

CHAPTER 8

The Doctor
at Lourdes

THE GREAT HEALING PROPERTIES OF Lourdes,
France, stem from the water of a spring that St. Bernadette
Soubirous in 1858 saw in an apparition and predicted
would cause many cures. Her other prophecies included
that there would be scientific achievements in harnessing
lightning, that terrible evil would come from Germany,
that man would one day walk on the moon, and that the
twentieth century would usher in an era of faith. Also
known as Bernadette of Lourdes, she had apparitions of a
young lady (later determined to be the Virgin Mary) who
asked for a chapel to be built in the nearby cave-grotto.
After a canonical investigation, her reports were deemed
worthy of belief. In 1909, a bishop exhumed her and found
that her body had not decayed. Pope Pius XI canonized
Bernadette as a saint in 1933, and the grotto went on to
become a major pilgrimage site. Each year, around three

million visitors—many with terminal medical conditions—visit Lourdes.

A century and a half after St. Bernadette's first visions, one of those visitors is a nun named Bernadette Moriau. Known as "Sister Bernadette," she comes to Lourdes on a pilgrimage from northern France. Her problems are as severe as they are many: She has compression of the nerve roots in the sacral region. She has bladder and rectal incontinence. She has intense pain. She is severely handicapped. She has been operated on three times and she has herniated discs. On top of all that, she has a genetic abnormality where the surgery she had on her back causes bad scars. She has a neuro bone marrow stimulator in place where bone-marrow-derived stem cells hopefully promote neurological recovery and decrease pain. Unfortunately the stimulator hasn't worked. She has cauda equina syndrome, severe lower back pain radiating down her legs due to clumping nerve roots. Her left foot has been deformed for more than two years, an equinus foot and ankle deformity, and she can barely move more than a few yards in her bedroom before she needs a wheelchair. She can only put weight on the front of the foot, not the heel, as her foot is stuck in a downward position. She has to do self-catheterization to avoid the stagnation of urine in her bladder. For years before coming to Lourdes she has been taking morphine in increasing doses.

In 2008 her family doctor encourages her to visit Lourdes. She is sixty-eight years old at the time, and she is exhausted. She believes in miracles, but she doesn't believe in a miracle for her.

While she doesn't think anything will come of the visit, she doesn't see why she shouldn't go. She attends all the religious services, including processions, masses, and blessings. But when she leaves Lourdes by the end of July, she is even worse than when she came.

&

AFTER ST. BERNADETTE Soubirous's death in 1879, an office of medical observation opened in Lourdes in 1883 to investigate the claims of medically unexplained cures. From the first apparition of Mary, seen by St. Bernadette, until today, the Medical Bureau of Lourdes has had more than 7,000 dossiers on healings, but has recognized only 70 of them as miracles.

The Vatican has strict criteria for determining medical miracles. For a cure to be recognized as medically inexplicable, first, the original diagnosis must be verified and confirmed, and second, it must be regarded as incurable with current treatments. When it comes to Lourdes, the cure must happen in association with a visit there, although drinking or bathing in the water from the site's springs is not required. The cure must be immediate (with rapid resolution of symptoms and signs of the illness) and complete (with no residual impairment). It also must be permanent.

Every cure is referred to the International Medical Committee of Lourdes (CMIL), an international panel of around twenty experts in various medical disciplines with differing religious beliefs. CMIL was created in 1954 and meets yearly with thirty members. Every one of its members investigates the case in question and immerses himself or herself in the medical literature about the condition. The committee relies on a rigorous process that includes being able to consult with other colleagues about the case. CMIL does not pronounce a cure miraculous; that can only be done by the Church. The Lourdes bureau may rule that a cure is "medically inexplicable."

A full investigation takes at least five years, in order to make sure that the cure is permanent. CMIL votes on each case and requires a two-thirds vote for the designation "inexplicable." Then the case is referred to the bishop of the diocese where the cured person lives. This bishop, in conjunction with his own experts and the Vatican, makes the decision whether the cure is "miraculous" or can still be refuted.

Dr. Alessandro de Franciscis is the president of the Lourdes Office of Medical Observations, a post he has held since 2009. Since taking on this role, he has seen three cases become the 68th, 69th, and 70th official miracles at Lourdes. He is a pediatrician and epidemiologist by training as well as a devout Catholic. With millions taking the Eucharist at Lourdes, de Franciscis believes in the True Presence of Jesus in the bread.

Dr. de Franciscis tells me in an interview that he has been coming to Lourdes for his entire life, beginning over fifty years ago. "I am Italian from Naples. The son of a mother born in Connecticut. I am following in a great tradition. There has been a residing physician in Lourdes since the year 1883. The first apparitions are before that in 1858. The first cure is recognized by the local bishop in 1862, and seven miracles are recognized by the bishop among the nine that his medical experts say are inexplicable. So in twenty years Lourdes becomes extremely famous in France and Belgium, and in 1881, there is total chaos here."

People were claiming to be cured by miracles and no one could verify them. This became a problem for the pastors of France. So the local pastor asked a doctor whom he knew to get involved. The doctor liked Lourdes and became the first residing physician. Now Dr. de Franciscis is the fifteenth, and the first who is not French.

"So what do I do in Lourdes? I sit here and wait for people to knock on my door, or write me a letter or an email. I can't give you exact numbers, but until Covid, between one hundred and one hundred ten alleged cures are reported to me every year."

There were zero alleged cures in 2021, because of the pandemic. Then, in 2022, there were more alleged cures. Dr. de Franciscis and his colleagues take claims of miracles seriously, and use high standards of medical examination and proof to evaluate them. "We use strict medical criteria," he says. "First, it is absolutely mandatory for us to have a precise diagnosis. Second, it has to be associated with a severe prognosis. Third, the cure must have happened unexpectedly. Fourth, the cure has to happen instantaneously. Fifth, it has to happen completely. And sixth, it has to last over time. And finally, the seventh and last criteria is that we have to have no other possible explanation. When people come to us allegedly being cured, we the bureau, the Constitutional

Office of Medical Observation, must determine this cure to be unexplained according to all current medical knowledge. We do follow the top medical journals, *The New England Journal of Medicine*, *Lancet*, etc., and we do understand that there are spontaneous regressions of severe diseases, but the strength of the method Lourdes uses compares to any other place of pilgrimage in determining whether the cure completely defies science or not.

"While all religions in the world may say that a person is miraculously cured of a disease, we may still call it a spontaneous remission," says Dr. de Franciscis. "We respect the opinion of a layman or nonbeliever, and the idea that one day we might explain a cure scientifically that we can't yet. On the other hand, we also command respect of the pastor of the person who establishes that a cure is in fact a true unexplained miracle."

❧

AFTER VISITING LOURDES, Bernadette Moriau returns to Bresles, by the little village near Bové, where she lives. She is so tired that she stays in bed for three days.

But after those three days, she finally feels strong enough to put all her clothes on again, including a rigid corset that keeps her neck still and a supportive orthopedic brace for her left deformed (equinus) foot, which is stuck in a downward position.

She goes to the chapel, and there finds nuns praying in silence; it is the Blessed Sacrament that Catholics believe invokes the presence of Jesus Christ. She also prays silently, and at one moment during the prayer, she realizes that at the same time of the afternoon five days before, in Lourdes, at the blessing of the Millards with the Blessed Eucharist, she felt that the presence of God was helping her to bear the weight of her handicap and her disease. In this moment, she remembers what she had experienced a few days before at Lourdes. She says, "I feel a voice inside of me that says, 'Detach all your apparatus, all your stuff.'" So she walks back to her room, and she detaches her rigid neck collar, which is made of steel and plastic, and she has no pain. For years she couldn't move her neck without excruciating pain. Now she can move it freely. Then she takes off her rigid steel and resin corset, and again, there is no pain.

She turns off her bone marrow stimulators and still there is no pain. She also takes off her foot brace and is able to move her foot. It is no longer immobilized. After self-catheterizing for years, she sits on a toilet for the first time and urinates. She starts crying so loudly that another nun who is passing the door enters the room and asks Bernadette what is happening. God has told her to throw away all her apparatuses, she says. And that evening, she stands and doesn't need the evening dose of morphine. She doesn't take it.

When someone stops opioids, there are supposed to be withdrawal symptoms, but Bernadette has none. The other nuns are so happy for her. The following morning, she walks three miles in the woods, then she goes to see her doctor. He sees her and starts crying, and they hug each other.

"I TAKE OFFICE at Lourdes in April 2009," Dr. de Franciscis tells me, "and this is my first big case. I call a meeting with all the doctors in Lourdes. Our tradition is to admit any doctor to our case discussion regardless of their spiritual, religious, or philosophical orientation. I have had a few Anglican non-Catholic Christians. I have been helped by the expertise of the chiefs of departments at various universities. With Bernadette I've seen and read the reports and the last images that were done. Remarkable. The doctors have all reviewed them. They say the lower spine operation she had was erroneous."

Dr. de Franciscis has many documents to verify these events. He also sends the case to thirty-three doctors and professors on the International Medical Committee of Lourdes to review all the facts, the medical records, the imaging studies before and after the cure. "Afterwards, I look meticulously for a super expert in southern France. Professor Jean Pouget reviews the case. At the time he is the chair of neurology at the medical school at the University of Marseilles and outgoing president of the French Society of Neurology. He agrees with all the details of the miracle and the complete resolution of the cauda equina syndrome."

Dr. de Franciscis is very affected by Sister Bernadette's case, saying that it is the most remarkable he's seen in his fifteen and a half years at Lourdes. He had officiated over the unexplained cure of the Italian nun Sister Luigina Traverso, which took place in 1965 and was declared the 68th Lourdes miracle in 2011. Luigina Traverso was wheelchair-bound after several operations for sciatica but started walking again after visiting Lourdes. De Franciscis then announced the 69th miracle in 2013, involving Mrs. Danila Castelli, who experienced the miracle in May 1989 of restored well-being despite multiple prior unsuccessful surgeries to remove a tumor near her bladder. But neither of these two prior miracles affected de Franciscis deeply the way the 70th miracle, of Sister Bernadette, does. "This is the only one that is recognized as an unexplained cure and goes on to be called a pure miracle, which is the second step. Of course, surgery from the back sometimes damages the nerve's roots. So how do we know that this isn't one of those cases? But the decompression of the spine which happens as a result of this unexplained cure is very, very rare. And then, her going back to normal life is absolutely unheard-of. She's been doing everything again for over ten years now. We are witnessing an extraordinary miracle cure."

Because his job is the job of a devil's advocate, Dr. de Franciscis sends Sister Bernadette to two different psychiatrists as well, to make sure she isn't somehow pretending to be cured. But Bernadette is found to be absolutely sane. She is a very enthusiastic person, with a gift in communicating. She is also a very pure and simple person.

She has a degree in nursing but had to quit after two years because of the excruciating pain. Now she wants to help others.

"I didn't study miracles in medical school," Dr. de Franciscis says. "Miracles remain an interpretation of the pastor of the cured person, which for us in our Catholic faith and in the Catholic Church is the bishop. So I don't know about miracles. My work here is simply to inform the bishop. For me it remains unexplained." Dr. de Franciscis approaches his job at Lourdes the same way he has always approached being a doctor. "I feel I'm just doing what I've always done in my life. I was in clinical medicine. I taught generations of residents pediatrics. I am just a contemporary physician with some academic training, able to understand if someone is truly sick and give a name to that using expertise. There's nothing more intelligent than saying I do not know, and asking someone who you believe knows more than you do to offer their expertise.

"A doctor's role is the same here as everywhere. To understand if a person is truly sick, to give a name to their disease, and to know if that person is truly cured. I think our duty is to understand: Is there a possibility that there might be a scientific explanation? In 2020, I went and examined all the hundred-plus reports here of alleged cures, the largest category being cancer, one-third of all the people who came to me. The same as you might see—gynecological, breast, prostate, and intestinal cancer."

De Franciscis pauses for emphasis. "Would you believe that *none* of these almost four hundred cases of alleged miracle cures of cancer have become a file that we are continuing studying in terms of how can we possibly defend it for no explanation in the medical field? None. Even if that patient had only the surgical ablation of the tumor, even if that patient had only one cycle of chemo or one cycle of immune therapy or whatever, radiotherapy, it can be defended as a scientific cure. There are none without a possible explanation.

All of these patients that came to me allegedly with miracle cures were all treated the way we do in allopathic Western medicine, and they don't qualify for the Church. They were found to be cured by science. I'm just a poor, simple doctor who approaches patients the way you do in New York and we do in France, in Italy."

I smile at Dr. de Franciscis's articulateness, at his wry irony, at his overt commitment to science. He is a man of faith, working at a place devoted to faith, and yet he doesn't compromise his medical principles one iota. This is important and believable. Dr. de Franciscis is humble, but I feel he is performing a great service. He lives and thrives at the great intersection between science and faith. He is patrolling the science but is conscious of the role and presence of the divine, even if he refrains from ruling on it and does not consider himself an expert on it. Still, the miracle cure of Sister Bernadette Moriau has clearly impacted him deeply, just as the apparitions of the Virgin Mary that came to St. Bernadette Soubirous over one hundred fifty years ago would impact millions when she asked for the original chapel to be built in the cave-grotto.

Dr. de Franciscis is fascinated by the mind/body connection and how it plays out in medicine and in life. "A mixture of the mind and the body, of the spiritual and the physical. But when it comes to the pure miracles of divine intervention without scientific explanation, that's decided by a bishop, not by a simple doctor like me. I am just looking for a diagnosis of a disease with a severe prognosis. And I help the Church say it was cured. There's a cure but no explanation. Take it from there.

"My mom, born in Connecticut, taught me and my sisters about miracles," Dr. de Franciscis says. "She sliced an apple, she sliced an onion, and she showed us the beauty of that perfect symmetry. She taught us as young children: This is the miracle. This is how God does it. Life itself is a miracle."

CHAPTER 9

Dodie Osteen and Her
World of Healing

THE YEAR IS 1981, AND Joel Osteen is an eighteen-year-old in college when his brother Paul calls him from the medical school at Oral Roberts University. "Mom is sick," Paul says.

Joel is instantly quite worried. Their mother, Dodie, has always been active and out in the yard. She is only forty-eight years old. But recently, Paul tells his brother, her skin has become yellow (jaundiced), she is weak, and she has lost twenty pounds. He wishes there was something he can do to help his mother but there isn't. She goes into the hospital for three weeks and is told she has terminal metastatic cancer with multiple lesions in the liver from an unknown primary site and likely has only a few weeks left to live. "There is nothing to do to help her medically or surgically," Paul says to me in an interview on SiriusXM.

At Christmas, Joel, Paul, their sister Lisa, and their father,

John, bring Dodie home for the holiday, and surprisingly, she doesn't go into a depression. Instead she is up and around with her children. She and husband John turn to prayer. Paul says that his parents "are lying on the floor in their bedroom and praying to God for Dodie." Paul prays with them. John finds a Bible there that happens to be opened to the book of Nahum in the Old Testament and the prophecy "Affliction shall not rise up the second time." John responds to this by praying to God and Jesus that Dodie is needed here on earth, that the church needs her and her children need her. Together they continue to pray for healing.

She is going forward through sheer will, Joel says to me in an interview. She is quoting scriptures from the Psalms of David, including "I will live and not die." From Jeremiah: "I will restore your health back onto you."

Lisa Osteen is also eighteen at the time of her mother's illness. She is the oldest daughter, and had overcome a crippling disease at birth similar to cerebral palsy after her parents prayed for her fervently. Lisa tells me that her mother was healthy her entire life before the sudden metastatic cancer of the liver diagnosis, where her weight drops down to eighty-one pounds. "Even though we are sad, we ask God for a miracle. Our parents had taught us the power of prayer and to look to Jesus as our healer. Our mother is given a few weeks to live, but she continues to live and get better little by little. She prays and quotes the scripture during the day and continues to work around the house, go to church, and pray for others. We witness the miracle working power of God."

Dodie continues to pray. She copies the Bible verses about healing and affixes them to a mirror, including these, from the New King James Version:

Exodus 23:25: "So you shall serve the Lord your God, and He will bless your bread and your water. And I will take sickness away from the midst of you."

Psalms 103:3: "Who forgives all your iniquities, who heals all your diseases."

Jeremiah 30:17: "For I will restore health to you and heal you of your wounds, says the Lord, 'because they called you an outcast saying: "This is Zion; no one seeks her."'"

James 5:14–15: "Is anyone among you sick? Let him call for the elders of the church, and let them pray over him, anointing him with oil in the name of the Lord. And the prayer of faith will save the sick, and the Lord will raise him up. And if he has committed sins, he will be forgiven."

Matthew 8:2–3: "And behold, a leper came and worshipped Him, saying, 'Lord, if You are willing, You can make me clean.' Then Jesus put out His hand and touched him, saying, 'I am willing; be cleansed.' Immediately his leprosy was cleansed."

Romans 8:11: "But if the Spirit of Him who raised Jesus from the dead dwells in you, He who raised Christ from the dead will also give life to your mortal bodies through His Spirit who dwells in you."

Nahum 1:9: "What do you conspire against the Lord? He will make an utter end of it. Affliction will not rise up a second time."

These are just some of the healing scriptures that Dodie Osteen relies on for her own deliverance from cancer, and will later utilize to help others who come to her to pray for cures.

"God can do what medicine can't," Joel says to me. As she continues to pray over time, she is believing something else is happening, refusing to give in to illness. She isn't going downhill. She is stabilizing. She still can't walk up steps, but the jaundice leaves her. Over the next few years, she gets better and better and better. There is no explanation for Dodie's healing other than divine intervention. The spontaneous regression of tumors in liver cancer is quite rare, occurring in one out of every 60,000 to 100,000 cases. "It doesn't work overnight, but slowly she begins to regain strength; her jaundice goes away," Paul says. "People just don't survive what she has, God heals my mother."

"From the time I am eighteen until I am thirty-six, my dad, a minister, preaches faith, prayer, healing, nonstop," says Joel. "He was raised a Baptist and started the Lakewood Church in a converted feed store on the outskirts of Houston in 1959, before I was born."

Dodie Osteen was the cofounder of the Lakewood megachurch with her husband, John. Lisa was born with an umbilical cord around her neck. They brought her home and found that she couldn't eat and was barely moving. So they prayed all night, and she got better and stronger, and was walking by her first birthday. Today she is healthy and is an associate pastor at Lakewood.

Dodie still stands at the pulpit at Lakewood Church and prays for the sick, continuing a ritual that has spanned decades and reached many thousands, with two services a week in English and one in Spanish. Millions more catch the services online.

Now ninety-one years old, Dodie believes God gives her these years to be the central part of the healing ministry at Lakewood. She spreads healing to others. She says all the time that something turned it around for her, and it can for you. She prays for fertility, for cancer cures, that God will bring someone a spouse. Every week someone comes to the church searching for God. One week, a forty-year-old gentleman comes from Atlanta. He has terminal cancer and two brokenhearted little girls. He prays with the Osteens on a Monday before going to the famous MD Anderson Cancer Center in Houston the following Tuesday for surgery. But when he gets there and they go in, they can't find the cancer.

"God turns situations around," Dodie says. "God is good. He is for us. Live in hope and faith."

When Dodie's husband, John, dies in 1999, Joel becomes the senior pastor, and he and his mother continue to pray for the sick. She lives a life of faith, and accepts each day as a gift, with God in control. She preaches that in order to get better, it helps to think to yourself that you are in fact getting better, that healing is flowing through you thanks to a personal God.

"God gives us our bodies," Joel says. "Physicians are the hands of God. But you have to hope, you have to choose to believe. We are known here for our hope. People come to us from everywhere to pray. We don't know how many are cured, but faith is the place to start as we ask God to intervene. When you don't believe, you cut off the chance of this. Your faith activates God's power."

✻

DR. PAUL OSTEEN is a vascular surgeon and medical missionary. He is also an associate pastor at Lakewood Church. He practiced surgery for many years in Little Rock, Arkansas, and now he spends almost half of the year in sub-Saharan Africa as a voluntary surgeon. Every year, Paul and his wife, Jennifer, conduct a two-day conference (Mobilizing Medical Missions, or M3) at the church, where health care professionals from around the globe come together to address health and community needs. He is an advocate and an organizer for humanitarian actions by US physicians to provide health care to vastly underserved areas, especially those in Africa.

Dr. Osteen discusses his experiences with medical miracles with me on the radio in January 2024. He emphasizes that in rural areas without extensive technology or health care infrastructure, he believes direct divine intervention is more visible.

"I can never forget my patient Buck Jones," he says. "He is in his early seventies when he develops jaundice and weight loss. The diagnosis is pancreatic cancer—a cancer, as you know, with a dismal prognosis. Many times, people don't live for even two years after diagnosis."

Dr. Osteen operates and removes all of the tumor, and then repairs the artery. This is a very big operation, and Buck is already weak and thin when it starts. Remarkably, he survives and even begins to gain strength. He also undergoes chemotherapy and receives radiation treatments. Dr. Osteen sees him back every few months for a couple of years, and he continues to be strong and healthy.

"What impresses me the most about Buck," Dr. Osteen says, "is his absolute joy at all times and his trust that he is in the palm of God's hand. Reminds me so much of my mother, Dodie, and her miracle recovery. He lives for twenty more years and dies of a heart problem, not of the cancer.

"Years later, Teresa Robinson comes into my hospital after a car accident. She is bleeding into her abdomen. She is losing a ton of blood and her blood pressure is very low. Her spleen is ruptured and I fix it, but she has torn the main veins behind her liver and she continues to bleed. There is nothing else I can do but pack the abdomen and close the wound and pray. There is little chance of survival. I take her to the ICU and tell her mother there is almost no chance. Her mom says, 'Thank you, Dr. Osteen, I'm going to go back to the chapel and pray.' That first night, blood continues to pour out of Teresa, but about eight hours later, she becomes warm, her blood pressure begins to stabilize, and she requires a little less blood every hour. Three months and five operations later and over one hundred units of blood and blood products later, Teresa leaves the hospital. I see her back many times and she is doing well. The last line of my operative report had said 'little chance of survival,' but then God took over."

Looking back on his mother's story, Dr. Osteen says he does not believe her case can be explained medically. "People just don't survive what she had," he says. "God healed my mother. Forty-four years after she gets a terminal cancer diagnosis, she is strong and healthy. An incredible miracle which she extends to others as God's vessel." With this deep belief in how God operates, Dr. Paul Osteen as a vascular surgeon and medical missionary guides others in his care. "I encourage my patients to pray even when all hope appears to be lost."

CHAPTER 10

Still Alive in the Hungarian Forest

CHANA LIVES IN THE ELEVENTH century BC. It is the time of the judges, before the first Temple is built in Jerusalem. She is one of the seven great prophetesses, married to Elkanah, who also has a second wife, Penina. Elkanah is known as a man of great character and piety who tries to bring his brethren closer to God.

Penina has seven children, while Chana is barren for nineteen years. But Chana prays to God for a son whom she vows she will devote to the service of God:

Then she made a vow and said, "O Lord of hosts, if You will indeed look on the affliction of Your maidservant and remember me, and not forget Your maidservant, but will give Your maidservant a male child, then I will give him to the Lord all the days of his life, and no razor shall come upon his head."

—1 SAMUEL 1:11 (NKJV)

Her prayer is granted and she gives birth to Shmuel, also known as Samuel, whom she turns over to Eli, the high priest. Samuel goes on to become a great prophet and an anointer of kings, including King David. Samuel is her miracle.

Chana's prayer for a child has influenced how Jews pray ever since. Her prayer demonstrates focused and careful devotion to God. When Chana prays, she is not praying about herself but about God. Efrem Goldberg, senior rabbi at the Boca Raton, Florida, synagogue and Torah scholar trained at Yeshiva University, tells me that when Chana prays, she is saying, "I *don't* want a child for selfish reasons; I want a child for Your reasons, dear God. I want my child to do good works, to redeem and repair to be an emissary of God." Chana teaches us that prayer should not be an instrument of selfishness. Her prayer is found in the book of prophets and is read as the Haftorah (which means "taking leave of" or "conclude"), following the Torah reading on the first day of Rosh Hashanah every year. It teaches people how to pray to God for another good year.

"When we pray to God," Rabbi Goldberg says, "He listens most closely and finds greatest favor when it is not about us, our ego, our pleasure or needs."

‫علم‬

HUNDREDS OF YEARS after Chana's prayer, Hezekiah, a direct descendant of King David, is king of Judah. He is one of the most righteous and faithful of all of Judah's kings and rules from 715 to 686 BC, beginning his rule at the age of twenty-five. He is the son of the wicked King Ahaz, an idol worshipper, and he is afraid to have an heir because he believes he too could turn from God (this ends up becoming true). But Hezekiah is the first king since David to keep the Lord's commandments and to teach his people to do the same. He also is king during an invasion of Judah by the Assyrians. As they are invading Jerusalem, Hezekiah is struck with a malignant and painful skin ulcer that is almost always fatal. According to the biblical scholar Rav Michael Feuer, who spoke to me in an interview, this affliction is God's punishment because of Hezekiah wanting to refrain from having children, because he knows that his son will go on to do bad things like his father did. God is angry at Hezekiah because he chafes against his fate. In fact, the Prophet Isaiah reveals to Hezekiah that the Lord says he should prepare to die from this affliction. According to Rav Feuer, Hezekiah says to Isaiah, "You can take your prophecy and go." Hezekiah turns his face to the wall away from Isaiah and prays directly to God, and God grants him fifteen more years as the infected sore heals. Hezekiah asks for a sign that he will be healed, and the sundial miraculously goes back ten degrees, another miracle in addition to his healing.

Rav Feuer says, "The lesson here is that direct prayer to God works and trumps prophecy. Human beings can bypass the prophecy through prayer."

Now that he remains alive, Hezekiah is able to hold off the 701 Assyrian invasion of Judah. He saves the city by expanding the walls of Jerusalem to the west, rerouting the springs, and bringing the water supply into the walls of the city, as God strikes down the Assyrian army with a plague and saves Jerusalem from being taken.

ﻋﻠﻢ

THE BRILLIANT RABBI Barry Mittelman, who has a PhD from Polytechnic Institute in Brooklyn, is an aging man with a kind face, a long salt-and-pepper beard, and eyes filled with the sharpness born of suffering. He believes that the miraculous story of his dear father, Isaac, reveals direct parallels to the biblical lessons of Chana and Hezekiah.

The story begins in Slovakia in November 1906, when Isaac (Ignatz) Mittelman is born. He is raised on a farm and later moves a few miles to Kosice, where as a young man he becomes the largest wheat dealer in the region.

Then, in 1938, Kosice is annexed to Hungary, and the Royal Hungarian Army occupies Kosice from 1938 to 1945. Antisemitic laws are imposed and Jews lacking Hungarian or Slovakian citizenship are imprisoned. Many Jews are deprived of jobs and properties. Kosice becomes one of the centers for the roundup and deportation of Jews.

It is 1940 when Isaac, his wife, his baby boy, and his wife's parents are rounded up in Kosice by the Royal Hungarian Army. Jewish families are typically concentrated before being deported, but Isaac is separated from his family and sent first to a forced labor camp in Sarospatak, Hungary (an hour drive south of Kosice). His family is taken to another camp. Like so many Jews, they are eventually sent to Auschwitz, in Poland, to die.

Some Jewish men are forced into military service, and many more are sent to forced labor camps, including Isaac. Before they are taken, Isaac and his brother bury a great sum of money in the basement of his brother's house to be retrieved after the war.

In 1942, the deportation of Jews to Poland starts as persecution in the region increases and all Jews lose income and property and are denied human rights. From 1943 to 1944, Isaac is sent to forced German labor camps in Belarus (Gomel, Brest-Litovsk, Pinsk, and Kobrin). In these camps he toils under slave labor conditions, working on bunker construction, digging trenches, and loading ammunition, all on little food. In mid-1944, Isaac is returned to Hungary, to the forced labor camp in Munkacs.

‫مله‬

IN MARCH 1944, German forces occupy Hungary. Wealthy Jews who are left are imprisoned and tortured to reveal where their possessions are hidden. Isaac is not there because he is already working at the forced labor camps. On April 27, 1944, all Jews are ordered to assemble in the three major synagogues; from there they are transferred temporarily to two brickwork factories on the outskirts of the city. There are 10,590 Jews in the brickworks. Working here does not spare Jews from the "final solution" of the Nazis, who directly occupy the expanded Hungary and send all remaining Jews to Auschwitz. Among them are Isaac's wife and child (who don't survive), as well as a woman who is a nanny for Isaac's child. The nanny will go on to become Isaac's second wife and Barry Mittelman's mother after the war.

☙

RABBI MITTELMAN SPEAKS softly, but if you listen closely, every word carries major impact.

"A miracle is something that's totally controlled by God. So if you want to take the biggest miracle of all, it's the splitting of the Red Sea. The miracle happens when one person actually jumps in. This is the test of it."

Mittelman says that God is performing miracles all the time, but the one he thinks about every day begins during Yom Kippur, on September 27, 1944, in Hungary.

It is a very cold day, below freezing at night. His father, Isaac, is interred in the labor camp at Munkacs and he is sure that his life is about to end.

The Hungarian soldiers catch him praying on Yom Kippur, the holiest day of the year, and for this, he is to be punished. So they hang him up, along with several others, from a tree in the freezing forest, hands tied around his waist, wrists bound very, very tightly.

"Luckily, my father is liked by the commandant," Rabbi Mittelman says. "So he gets punishment number two. Number one is where they put a rope around you, and one side is pulled by one truck and one by another truck, and they pull you completely apart."

It is below zero in the Hungarian forest. In the morning, when they cut them all down, only Isaac is still moving.

Rabbi Mittelman says that it shows God has a purpose for what his father will do later on. It isn't yet his time. God hears Isaac's prayer on Yom Kippur and spares his life much as he once spared King Hezekiah's.

Also like Hezekiah, Isaac suffers from a skin wound that should kill him, but doesn't. "He has an infection on his fingers because they also tied up his wrists to be very tight, and he doesn't have any circulation to his hands," Rabbi Mittelman says. "And then they take him to the nearby hospital, really they are supposed to amputate the three middle fingers on his left hand, the tips and two of his knuckles. But the reason they decide to let him live after he survives the night becomes clear: They will torture him, experiment with him out of pure cruelty, those horrible people in the hospital. They literally don't do anything at all until the infection spreads all the way to his elbow. Finally, when they have pushed it to the point where the infection will likely kill him, they decide to amputate. They put a towel between his teeth to bite on, no anesthesia, just a towel to bite on. It is probably a dirty towel, and they operate. They stitch up the stump of his arm and he is recuperating. No meds for pain. It is very slow and challenging."

Isaac Mittelman is transferred to the Royal Hospital of Szeged. He continues to receive minimal care. Meanwhile, the Allied bombings continue throughout Hungary.

And then all of a sudden, one day there is bombing at the hospital. Isaac says the Shema prayer, "Hear, o' Israel, the Lord is God, the Lord is one." And when he finishes, just as he shouts, "The Lord is one," the bombing stops.

"Just like that, God answers his prayer again," says Rabbi

THE MIRACLES AMONG US

Mittelman. "God is responding to a direct appeal from my father. He looks around. Everyone is dead. All patients, all doctors, nurses and orderlies too. Everyone. My father's bed is in the corner, and the ceiling is totally collapsed; the entire building collapses right up to where his bed is. His bed is maybe two, three feet away from the collapse. And he is the only one still alive."

Isaac grabs fatigues from a dead Hungarian soldier in the waiting room so that now he looks like a soldier who was wounded at the war front. He speaks Hungarian fluently and makes his way to Budapest. There he survives the rest of the war in his disguise. Budapest has a rule that any soldier who comes back from the war wounded gets first servings of water and bread rations. Isaac is the first one to get food and supplies, and he doesn't have to prove anything because he comes without an arm, and he says he lost it in battle. He goes in and out of different hospitals receiving better care than others until his arm finally heals.

Isaac survives for nine months until the Allies rescue him. They don't shoot at him because in addition to Hungarian and German, he also speaks Yiddish. He calls out in Yiddish and they know right away that he is not an enemy.

༄

RABBI MITTELMAN SAYS that after the war, his father, Isaac, literally starts a new life. His wife and first child were gassed in Auschwitz in the latter part of the war, and his niece is the only one who survives.

126

Immediately after the war, Isaac goes back to his brother's house, where they buried the money years before. But when he attempts to go down to the basement where the stash is buried, he gets sick to his stomach, because the walls are plastered with human blood where his brother and mother and the rest of the family were shot. Isaac leaves without digging up the stash. He simply can't bear it. But he does find the receivables book of money owed to his business from the area bakeries, and he goes to all of them to collect.

Isaac emigrates to New York City, where he becomes a Mashgiach, which is a kosher supervisor, for the city's largest catering hall in the 1950s. It is called the Riverside Plaza Hotel, and it has six ballrooms and six affairs functioning simultaneously.

"My father after the war continues to show that he is a very, very honest, honorable man. He is a very religious man. He becomes even more religious after the war, because he feels indebted to God. That God saves him. Surviving the night from that tree is one miracle. His saying the Shema when the bombing hits is the other."

Rabbi Mittelman also says that his father's left arm healing miraculously from an infected sore and a hideous amputation in the hospital run by the Nazis after hanging in the frozen Hungarian forest all night brings back the memory of Hezekiah and his miraculous healing from his open ulcer. Both men pray directly to God, and God responds. By not running away from what God has in store for them, both men invoke the power of God to save them.

To this day, these miracles reverberate in Rabbi Mittelman's

heart. Barry recalls the central role his father played throughout his childhood. "My father was my guiding light. I never
made a big decision in life unless I passed it by him first. He
would give me his blessing and I would continue on to God.
When I am six years old I ask my mommy why Daddy doesn't
have a left arm, and she says he was born that way. She doesn't
tell me the whole story until I am sixteen years old. Thinks I
am too young to hear it."

At this, Rabbi Mittelman begins to cry. He understands
deeply that his father Isaac's story demonstrates that there is
a personal God who answers prayers even in the most horrible time in history, perhaps because it is the most awful time.
"This is what the Torah is all about," Rabbi Mittelman says.

"My father is the descendant of a great rabbinical dynasty.
As a Mashgiach, one day he receives an order of chickens
whose wholesale price is twenty-five thousand dollars. Opening crate after crate, inspecting the chickens, he discovers
that they are perfectly clean, without a stray hair on any. He
tells the driver he is not accepting delivery. The driver freaks
out, calls his boss, who offers my dad five thousand dollars
as a bribe to accept the order. My father throws him out with
the chickens and is then thrown out of the union. After a few
days it is found that the chickens, after their halachic [Jew-
ish law] slaughter, are passed through a hot-water process for
the easy cleaning and removal of their hairs. But this ren-
ders them halachically unkosher. My father is immediately
rehired as a master Mashgiach and never questioned again."

Isaac's success and many grandchildren and great-
grandchildren stand in defiance of the wishes of the Nazis.

He lives to ninety years old and continues to advise others. "People come to him to get his advice on their issues and problems. He is like a Hasidic rebbe without the dress regalia."

Rabbi Mittelman says that his father is one of the few Holocaust survivors who retain their full religious beliefs as Orthodox Jews despite what they were forced to endure. His miraculous survival fuels his belief in God.

One morning, Isaac's best friend from childhood, Rabbi Weiss, visits him for Shabbat. The man is very important in the Jewish community, a judge in the Jewish court. Isaac Mittelman hosts him in his home, brings him to the synagogue, and has a big meal in his honor, but then discovers him sitting alone smoking a cigarette. The then-young Barry Mittelman observes the conversation from the doorway.

"You know you can't smoke on Shabbat!" says Isaac.

"Who cares?" the judge says. "I don't believe anymore in this God. How can I? I lost a wife and two of my children to the gas chamber."

"But you are a rabbi and a judge in the Jewish court. How can that be? How can you not believe?"

"I am just going through the motions to make a living," Rabbi Weiss says.

"I am very sorry for you," Isaac Mittelman says. "But if you insist on making fire on Shabbat, you will have to leave. I am still your dear friend and I will still see you, but I can't have you dishonoring our God."

Surviving against all odds, Isaac's faith is unwavering. With all he has endured, he could be like the judge and give up, but instead he sees his own life as a testament to God's presence, and he needs to honor that every day. As with Chana so many centuries before, with Isaac Mittelman God is answering a prayer for a life who will go on to do important deeds in the world. He survives in order to fulfill God's plan for him.

But Rabbi Mittelman adds that while Chana's prayer is for a new life, his father's prayer on Yom Kippur (Viddui, the confession) is preparing for death. And again in the hospital: "When he says the Shema in the hospital as it is being bombed, he thinks it is a death confessional. Life is over. But God spares him. God hears his prayer and responds. He does not expect to live but he does." Rabbi Mittelman compares this to the biblical story of the great King Hezekiah, "who also expects to die but is saved by a medical miracle and divine intervention."

CHAPTER 11

Dr. Ellay Hogeg-Golan

ELLAY HOGEG-GOLAN IS A PHYSICIAN. She is thirty-four years old and a graduate of Ben Gurion Medical School in Beersheba, Israel. From there she launched her training in anesthesiology and ICU medicine with an internship at Soroka Medical Center, also in Beersheba. In Israel and here in the US, specially trained anesthesiologists are playing a larger and larger role in managing acutely ill patients. No one can manage an airway or a ventilator better or with more alacrity than a critical care anesthesiologist. They nimbly respond to sudden changes in pressure and oxygen and save lives. Ellay is really looking forward to this career.

Unfortunately, her essential training and her life are both severely interrupted seven months into her internship.

It is 6:30 a.m. on October 7, 2023. She is still at home at her small house on the Kfar Aza kibbutz near the Gaza border with her husband, Ariel, and their eighteen-month-old daughter, Yael.

She hears the missiles. She does not know it at the time,

but by the end of this day she will be on the very ventilator she has been training to manage.

She doesn't panic. It isn't that unusual to hear rockets, but there are a lot of them going off at once. When she hears the rat-tat-tat of machine gun fire, she knows this is something much bigger. Her phone begins buzzing with unimaginable messages.

COME AND HELP ME. THEY SHOT ME.

Her husband also realizes this is something very bad. He grabs two kitchen knives. He takes water and fruit for their daughter. They go into their "safe room," their daughter's room at the back of the house. Her husband leans a small cabinet against the door to keep it closed.

"Prevention," he says.

They stay in this closed room for hours. They hear a lot of weapons going off. Firing. Shots. Screams.

Before attending medical school, Ellay had been a troop commander in the Israel Defense Forces (IDF). She'd trained other soldiers in how to prepare for combat. She finished high school around the time that Israel was withdrawing from southern Lebanon, so she didn't have to go there. She remembers going to Gaza as a child, when things were much better. She returned to Gaza as a troop commander years later to help deal with "skirmishes."

Her husband, Ariel Golan, also thirty-four years old, knows he will remember this horrible disaster as the worst day of their lives. He's getting WhatsApp messages like

"They're here. Someone please help me." It's terrifying. The electricity is off. They wait.

At 7:30 a.m., Ariel learns that his dear friend Aviv is wounded, by way of a text from his wife. His house is just a hundred yards away. Ariel starts to plan in his head for worst-case scenarios. They must keep their daughter alive no matter what. They get messages that hundreds are being killed. Aviv's wife texts again, "Please, can someone come help him." Ellay wants to go help, as any doctor would. She gets her stethoscope and her bag, but another friend texts that there are twenty terrorists outside. Ariel convinces her not to go. They know Aviv won't make it now. People are dying all over their neighborhood. Fourteen people fight back against the terrorists and get to the armory, but there are thirty terrorists there waiting.

If Ellay had gone, she would have been killed immediately.

Six hours after the attack began, someone rattles the door. They are inside the house, trying to open the shelter door. The cabinet Ariel has put there is holding it closed.

"Come out. Give us jewelry. Give us money. Come on, come out," they entreat them. Ellay knows everyone out there is Hamas. She doesn't believe anything they say. They aren't Nukhba; they aren't the troops. They are civilian Hamas. She hears Arabic being spoken right outside their window. The fight of their life has started. They are in the dark, and Hamas is outside in the light. They can see them.

"Come with us," they say. "We aren't going to harm you."

For ten minutes they try to negotiate to get Ellay and her family to come out.

"Take what you want," she says. Hamas is in the living room, in the bedroom. The cabinet blocking the door is the only barrier between life and death. They don't try to get inside the little shelter room yet. Ellay sends text messages to her family. What she needs is the army. Where is the army? Ariel calls Ellay's parents on the other side of the kibbutz.

"Send someone to save us. They are here." Ariel is calm, methodical, even in his speech. Ellay's parents are in their safe room on the other side of the kibbutz, trying to survive too.

Soon the phones run out of batteries. The battle seems lost.

Hamas fires what feels like hundreds of bullets at the door. Then smoke starts to come through the doors. They keep the window to the safe room closed and hold the cabinet against the door, but it's clear the Hamas raiders have set fire to the house.

The Golans are inhaling smoke and can't breathe. They run out of the safe room through the fire. Hamas sees them through the flames and throws glass bottles, wood, and rocks. Ariel protects his family with a mattress. Then Hamas throws a gas tank into the fire. A flame torch. Ariel can see they are going to be burned alive.

Ellay and Ariel stuff clothing into their mouths and nose, but they start to suffocate from the smoke.

Ellay gets them up and to the shower in the other room. They wet themselves down. Ellay knows as a doctor that this may limit some of the damage to their burning skin. The shelter is made of cement. It does not burn, but it heats quickly, like an oven.

They can hear Hamas outside the house now, waiting by the shelter window.

If the family comes out, they will be killed.

They decide not to go outside. They will deal with the fire no matter what and not leave. Better to die from the fire than at the hands of Hamas. They put their tiny daughter between them and cover themselves with a mattress. They wait as their house burns, and then their bodies burn.

The house starts to give way.

What happens next is very difficult to believe. They go to the living room. They take out some kitchen knives. They will fight them to the death. The house is engulfed in flames. But at this point Hamas just leaves. They try to steal a car, but they can't figure out the code to get it started. So they just leave.

Ellay says, "Let's go," so they go too.

Ellay and her family jump out of the living room window. They have no food, no water, and no clothes. They have only their wounds and burned underclothes.

It feels like a miracle that they kept Hamas out of the safe room, another miracle that they escape just as the house collapses.

They start to run away from the house. As far away as they can go. Hamas could be anywhere. They run, limping, with burns over much of their bodies, to the agricultural part of the kibbutz. They have no shoes. They hide behind bushes and rocks. Ellay knows they're getting so much dirt in their wounds, they are going to get infected.

"We walk all the way to the other side of the kibbutz,"

Ariel says. "I am wearing boxers, no shoes; Ellay has on a T-shirt; Yael is in a diaper. We are mostly naked."

Across the fields they see a big tractor, a harvesting machine looming at them as a sign from God, and they head for it, not knowing what they will find next.

The tractor is next to a cabin. First they hide under it in a sack. Then they slowly crawl out and find a ladder. They climb up high in the cabin, find a room up at the top, and wait.

"We wait for an hour and a half," Ariel says.

Their daughter begins to cry, to whimper. Ellay knows she is in bad pain, but she is also badly dehydrated. She knows this as a doctor. Burn victims lose fluid. So she breastfeeds her daughter, and she starts to quiet.

After an hour and a half, her baby Yael falls asleep.

"By three p.m., Yael is losing consciousness and we know we need to get help. Ellay has been breastfeeding her the whole time or she would be gone."

They are worried they can't stay in any one place for too long. They climb down and start to walk, to stumble really, to the gate of the kibbutz. They don't know who they will meet along the way. "We run to the front of the kibbutz, to the entrance. Hamas is everywhere, but somehow we make it." When they get to the entrance, there are people there, so they hide. They fear they have come all this way for nothing. Then Ellay and Ariel see they are Israeli soldiers.

The soldiers take them to the next kibbutz and then to a gas station, where they are lifted away on a helicopter with the IDF. They are taken directly to the burn unit at Sheba

Medical Center, just outside Tel Aviv. It is only then, as the adrenaline and fear dissipate, that they realize how hurt and burned they are.

Ellay calls her father and they cry together. Her parents make it out too.

Ariel tells me that he doesn't think in terms of miracles. "This is our will to live. Our need to save our daughter. Still, we are incredibly fortunate that my wife has breast milk to keep our baby hydrated, that the terrorists we meet are not armed, and that there is a helicopter two minutes away. Ellay is the strongest woman I have ever met. I have always known this. She proves it on October seventh as we save our family. Three out of three of us."

As they get off the helicopter at Sheba, Ellay can barely breathe. She is severely dehydrated. Her lungs are burned. She passes out from all the pain.

She and her family are put into medically induced comas so they can be treated. Burn wounds are too excruciating to treat otherwise.

PROFESSOR JOSEF HAIK is a plastic surgeon. He is the director of the burn center at Sheba Medical Center, one of the best burn centers in the world, and he is also the head of the Department of Plastic and Reconstructive Surgery at Sheba.

Haik is in charge of Ellay Hogeg-Golan's remarkable recovery. "Some plastic surgeons think they are God or God's messengers," he says. "I don't see it like that. I am just doing my job, treating people the best I can."

When he sees Ellay and her family in the ER, they are in bad shape. Sixty percent of Ellay's body is covered with burns. Ariel is 50 percent covered. The baby, Yael, has burns over 30 percent of her body. Ariel also has a significant inhalation injury.

"They had inhalation injuries from the fire, from the smoke," Haik says. "A miracle that they survived at all."

Yael has more problems than burns. She had been sick at the kibbutz before the attack, and now she tests positive for COVID. They put her on the ventilator right away. Yael is moved to the pediatric ICU. Luckily, kids are more resilient. She is treated conservatively, and Dr. Haik knows soon that she will heal.

He uses NexoBrid on all three, a miracle drug, in the place of standard surgical debridement, which cuts off more tissue. "NexoBrid only removes dead tissue so the scars will be better." All three have burns ranging from superficial to deep, partial to full thickness. Ariel tests positive for COVID too and then turns negative. Ellay tests negative but then turns positive.

Dr. Haik says Ellay is worse than the others, but she is more worried about her husband and her daughter. Haik is more worried about Ellay. "I can see from the beginning that this is more than just burn injuries."

According to Professor Haik, Ellay and her family's positive outcome has a lot to do with being treated with NexoBrid immediately upon arrival at Sheba. NexoBrid was developed by the company MediWound and was first approved for use in Israel in 2014. It targets and dissolves nonviable burned tissue resulting from severe burns, leaving healthy tissue alone. NexoBrid is a topical biologic drug that uses proteolytic enzymes enriched in a chemical called bromelain, extracted from the stems of pineapple plants. The enzymes specifically target debris from dead or dying cells. NexoBrid is applied to a clean, moist wound area after mixing the powder with a gel. It is used to treat deep partial-thickness and full-thickness thermal burns.

More recently, its use has spread to the rest of the world. The US Food and Drug Administration approved NexoBrid for the treatment of thermal burns in adults in December 2022. In August 2024, the FDA expanded the approval to include pediatric patients.

As Haik says, this advance decreases the need for surgical debridement and skin grafts, and most of all it creates a boundary for the surgeon so they don't inadvertently cut through healthy tissue. Healing is easier and occurs more rapidly. NexoBrid is a miracle of modern medicine.

مر

AFTER A WEEK, Ariel and Yael awaken from their comas. Unfortunately, Ellay's case is much more complicated.

Her COVID is severe. She is treated with antiviral drugs and steroids. She develops blood clots (deep vein thrombosis and pulmonary embolus) and is treated with blood thinners. She needs a long stay in the respiratory ICU—her lungs are overwhelmed with inhalation injury, COVID, and blood clots. Her immune system is suppressed from the burns and she can't fight off infection. She develops a fungal skin infection, probably from the spores that get into her wounds under that harvesting machine. Dr. Haik needs to directly debride areas of her skin that are infected with a fungus, known as fusarium. It spreads to the already badly damaged lungs. He treats her for weeks with antifungal drugs. There is a high mortality rate from this infection, but she barely manages to fight it off.

Her management on the ventilator is extremely difficult. An amazing team of critical care specialists takes care of her, just as she one day intends to take care of others in similar circumstances. The head of the intensive care unit, Dr. Yael Haviv-Yadid, takes a strong personal interest in her recovery. Dr. Haviv was instrumental in Israel's strong response to COVID and was in charge of the COVID units throughout the pandemic, setting precedent and protocol for the rest of Israel and the world. She is a leader in ICU medicine. Ariel meets with Dr. Haviv many times during his wife's months in the ICU, and he describes this doctor to me as "sensitive, a great human being, she makes you feel good by explaining the situation so you can understand it. She translates for normal people. She thinks Ellay is going to make it. She gives me hope. She knows Ellay is going into the same field of medicine and sees herself as Ellay's guardian angel."

Haik has never treated such a horrific combination of a big burn, COVID, inhalation injury, a big pulmonary embolus, and the fungal infection before. He calculates the risk of death as extremely high.

Haik thinks to himself that if she does not survive, he will resign. Ellay is a doctor, and he and the team have to do better than their best for her. It's a miracle she's made it this far, he thinks. He can't let a miracle go to waste.

Somehow, she survives. His team cultures some of her cells to use for skin grafts, but then she heals without grafts, partly due to the NexoBrid.

"God doesn't think He's a surgeon," Haik says to me. "I'm humble. I do my job. I hope I do it well. Some surgeons think they are God, but not me."

Over three months after October 7, Dr. Haik and others will treat over 1,600 patients here at Sheba, including 250 with severe injuries from the war, including burns and gunshot wounds.

"Right after the attack, I am shocked and depressed like everyone, but I know I have to soldier on. My kids and part of my team here go to the war. I am kind of alone, but life goes on. I still have to treat melanoma and breast cancer every day on top of the war injuries, trauma, rehab, neurosurgery, while at the same time worrying about my family. This worry translates into more empathy for the patients I am taking care of at Sheba."

❧

"I AM IN an induced coma for ten days," Ariel says to me. "The first time I am able to see my daughter is on the twenty-fifth of October. I couldn't see her with open burns. I didn't want to pass infection to her. It is so hard for me to see my little baby with burns all over her face and arms and legs. I am so emotional, so destroyed. I am so upset that Yael was on the ventilator for eight days. When we are united, we sleep in the same room. Seeing me makes her feel so much better, and me too. Yael was able to walk at ten months, but not in the ICU, but when she sees me she starts to walk and talk again.

"I cannot see Ellay for ten days after I wake up. Because of the smoke inhalation and the risk of infection. The first time is October twenty-seventh; she has the tracheostomy in her neck and they are bringing her back to the burn unit. I see her through the window. She is starting to wake up. But then she gets bad again and they have her on ECMO [extracorporeal membrane oxygenation], where her chance of dying is more than fifty percent. I always believe Ellay will make it. I know how strong she is. I don't give negative thoughts a chance."

علم

AFTER FIFTY-THREE DAYS in a coma, Ellay starts to wake up. She has been having severe nightmares whenever they try to wake her. Weaning her off the ventilator is very difficult. When they lower the settings and taper down her analgesics and sedatives, her heart rate and blood pressure go up—from nightmares, hallucinations—and they have to pull back.

While she is still in her coma, she dreams that people are chasing her, killing her, kidnapping her. In her dreams, it feels real. She is filled with visions. She feels like she is in an episode of *Black Mirror*, the British TV show about unease and uncertainty in the modern high-tech world. In one dream she is in a big factory, with terrorists chasing her. Capturing her, they put her in a vending machine. "They wrap me up," she tells me later. "I am a snack, like an M&M, and people can buy me later. I think this is one of my last dream hallucinations before I wake up."

When she finally wakes up, she thinks it has only been five days. She doesn't know about Hamas. She doesn't know that 55 people from her kibbutz were murdered out of 765 residents and that 22 more were kidnapped.

Dr. Haviv keeps Ellay on the ventilator to protect her. The ICU team converts it to a tracheostomy tube in her neck because of the inhalation injury, the blood clots, the disorientation.

"My husband is in a coma for a week," Ellay says to me. "I am in a coma for fifty-three days; the doctors and nurses fight for my life every single day using every tool they have at Sheba. The leader is Dr. Yael Haviv. I come to admire her and think that it is no simple coincidence that she has the same name as my daughter."

Haik knows her family is from Morocco; she is Sephardic, and has tight skin that tends to scar much more easily, a Fitzpatrick classification IV (brown skin, brown hair, and brown eyes). He vows to stay ahead of the scarring with preventive laser treatments on top of the miracle of the extremely successful NexoBrid treatments.

When she finally does recover, Haik's team is so impressed

with her strength and courage that they offer to continue her training in ICU and internal medicine here at Sheba.

ﻣﻌﻲ

DR. HARATS MOTI is the head of the Israeli National Burn Center and runs the burn unit ICU at Sheba. On October 7, 2023, Moti is called to the army, where he works as a platoon commander stationed in Gaza. When he returns, in December, Ellay is just waking up, and Moti then participates in her care as she transitions from acute management to rehab. He reports directly to Dr. Haik.

"The whole story is a miracle," Moti says, speaking to me from Sheba Medical Center. "She is so resourceful, how she gets out of the kibbutz and makes it to the hospital. From the beginning she is bad, recovering from COVID, with an inhalation injury from the fire, a big pulmonary embolus, needing oxygen, needing ECMO, treated for fungus, on the ventilator for fifty-three days.

"She has big burns, deep, huge patches over the body, sixty percent, mostly her torso. Partial and complete thickness. Such a severe burn, it cannot be taken for granted that this person can survive. They induce coma because of the need for painful treatment in the beginning and so they can control the breathing. It takes a lot of time for her to get out of recovery and for her body to get stronger and back to reality."

Moti calls NexoBrid a game changer. "With the scalpel you never know when to stop cutting. Whereas the enzyme only removes dead tissue. You can actually see the burn death.

144

"We use coma and sedation for a long time when treating big burns like this," Moti says. "We worry a lot about infection especially with the big dirty wounds and the weakened immune system."

Moti says that Ellay's motivation is a direct determiner of the final outcome. "Once she is out of the coma, there is a huge emotional and physical struggle. Ellay has much support, and there is an advantage in being a smart physician in that she understands exactly what is happening to her. But there is also a big downside. She knows what there is to overcome. Awareness can also work against a physician who is also a patient."

At Sheba, the medical doctors co-manage patients like Ellay with the burn specialists in terms of ventilators, treatment of infection, and blood clots. They all find Ellay to be a person of great character and strength. "She does not give in to the frustration of a breathing tube in her neck or of a long rehabilitation," Moti says.

After October 7, while Moti travels back and forth from the hospital to the war, his boss, Professor Haik, is overwhelmed with many kinds of injuries but does not waver. "He is a great physician," Moti says.

☙

PROFESSOR HAIK SPEAKS to me about Ellay's arduous rehab process. "We like to say, 'We dress and God heals.' Obviously rehab after such burns takes a long time. She goes to rehab here and most of it is done at the beginning over the first two or three weeks in house and then in Bay Hospital rehab. And she starts her internship while she is still with pressure garments and silicone sheets and occupational and physical therapy. We send her as soon as possible to return to everyday activities, and to return to her family."

Silicone scar sheets promote healing and improve the appearance of burns, decreasing redness and improving hydration to the scar site, which interferes with the deposition of collagen and makes the whole scar less bumpy and less pronounced.

Haik says the goal of rehab after such severe burns is to stretch the skin out, "to get full range of motion, to learn to walk again. She does incredibly well with the program. She needs to gain strength again due to the muscle consumption from the burn. She wears pressure garments, the silicone sheets, lasers to prevent and treat scars. Even metabolic rehabilitation is needed because it takes a long time after to go back to normal metabolism."

I have never thought in terms of metabolic rehabilitation until Haik mentions it, but the fact is, severe burn injury causes a prolonged hypermetabolic state with a massive amount of tissue breakdown. Treatment with high-carbohydrate formulas is crucial. "Metabolic rates of burn patients can surpass twice normal, and failure to fulfill these energy requirements causes impaired wound healing, organ dysfunction, and susceptibility to infection. Adequate assessment and provision of nutritional needs is imperative to care for these patients."

THE FINAL STAGE of Ellay's rehabilitation is not what Dr. Haik or the rest of the staff at Sheba Medical Center are hoping for. They are so inspired by her recovery and the fact that she is able to complete her internship while rehabbing at the same time that they really want her to stay and complete her residency here at Sheba. Haik has grown very fond of Ellay and her family.

And Ellay is honored to be asked. It is a great anesthesia/critical care program at the top trauma center in the entire region. But now that her physical recovery is almost complete, she finds that the final part of her *emotional* recovery is to return to the place she started and reassume the reins of her career there, training to be a critical care specialist in the image of Dr. Haviv, who saved her from severely damaged lungs with expert management. It was almost inconceivable that her lungs could recover from the burns combined with the clots, the COVID, and the invasive fungus, but they have. She can breathe again without difficulty. Returning to Beersheba is her final milestone. "Yes, I am finishing my internship here at Sheba Hospital and doing the final rehab and then going back to Soroka in November to complete my residency there."

Ellay will carry the lessons learned from her tortuous recovery with her for the rest of her life. "Now I understand what it is like to be a patient. My family is with me every single day, helping me to understand the situation and recover. I understand that this is the meaning of my job as a physician, to bring people hope, and I am eager to embrace it. When a situation is bad, it can be made better."

Ellay ponders the meaning of God and the role God plays in her survival and recovery. "Coming from a reform family, I am not always used to thinking in these terms, but as I tell my mother, God saves you. If you give to God, God saves you. I don't believe God was there during the bad situation when Hamas attacked, but now, God is here and He is helping me, helping us. He put us here and He gives us the strength to create and destroy life.

"It's the people's fault, that brought us this situation where we keep fighting all the time. I believe that people did it, brought us here. These people were evil outside of the house, because of the hate. In that day, they came to take life, to destroy us. As a doctor I am helping people to recover, to save life, the opposite of the terrorists. God has given me the strength to keep going, to recover as a family, as a country."

Throughout Israel, doctors treat all comers, whether they are Jews or Arabs, Palestinians, or even terrorists. Doctors are trained to treat all who are ill or wounded, and they do so without hesitating. "I studied medicine with Arabs, with Christians, with Jews," Ellay says. "You work with people, not religions. I hope the hospital I work at, Soroka, will be in the world of recovery, so we can work together, combine our strength together, to save people just as I was saved.

"I am going to therapy," Ellay tells me. "It is helping me a lot, and my daughter is helping me a lot. I have a little bit of PTSD. My daughter gives me strength. She is my joy; she keeps me going. I am back at work and that helps too. It takes time. They took my community, my body, and I am not going to give them my hope and my dream. I am going to go back as a family and a doctor. I have returned to my residency, first at Sheba and then at Soroka. Giving back to patients, what they [Hamas] took from me.

"They came to take life; it is so meaningful that I am going to save life as a doctor.

"We made it; we will go on in our lives. Our little family of three. We are still recovering. We live now close to Tel Aviv—we found an apartment close to the hospital; there is a kindergarten for our daughter. She started there when I was sedated. We are still living here now. But we will go back and I will go back to Soroka. I have scars all over my body and I still wear pressure suits for the burns. I still get laser treatments. Recovery is still a long time."

CHAPTER 12

Montgomery MD

WHEN DR. ROBERT MONTGOMERY CAME to NYU Langone Health in 2016 to start a new Transplant Institute, he didn't know he would be assembling a team that would eventually be giving *him* a heart transplant.

Robert Montgomery has dealt with life-threatening heart problems for years. It starts when he is a surgical intern at Johns Hopkins back in the 1980s. His brother Richard suddenly dies at just thirty-five years of age while waterskiing. Their father had died young as well of a dilated cardiomyopathy when young Bob was a teen. Now he has his brother's heart sent to a pathologist at Hopkins, fearing there's a genetic problem in his family. He is right. His deceased brother also had a cardiomyopathy.

Bob realizes that his father's problem wasn't isolated. So Bob and his remaining older two brothers sign up for stress tests, where you run on a treadmill while readings are taken. It turns out Bob's brother Larry has pretty advanced heart dysfunction and will need a heart transplant. Bob seems lucky. He has pretty well-preserved heart function. But on the treadmill he develops ventricular tachycardia, a life-threatening dysrhythmia.

He is just twenty-nine years old.

His cardiologist tells him he's at high risk to die at any time. The good news is that he can get a recently invented implantable defibrillator. It can shock him back into normal rhythm if needed. The bad news is that he can't be a surgeon. Surgeons constantly use high-voltage tools to cauterize blood vessels. If the defibrillator kicks on while he is handling the tools, he could shock the patient as well as himself. He decides to get the defibrillator.

The chair of surgery suggests he go into research, at least at first, and not leave medicine altogether. Robert Montgomery is very grateful for the positive attitude and support of the chair of surgery at Hopkins, and he decides to follow his advice.

He heads to Oxford University to work with Sir Peter Morris, who is doing world-class transplant research. He enrolls in a PhD program in molecular immunology.

Dr. Montgomery starts to think of ways to combine his training, and it all leads in one direction: transplantation.

"My work at Oxford is in transplant rejection and also in thymus development, how the thymus educates our immune system. My thesis is on that and I am thinking that if I can't do surgery, at least I now have a pathway to at least stay in the game of transplantation.

"Right after I have the device put in, and I am over in Oxford, I learn there is only one cardiologist in the entire UK who can test the defibrillator. It is an experimental device."

Dr. Montgomery sees this cardiologist, but he is unable to receive clearance to resume his surgical training. He also lives in fear that the device will go off at any moment.

One day a terrible car accident happens in front of his house. The car is upside down. He crawls through a window to extricate a baby who is unconscious. His adrenaline is spiking as he tries to save this baby, and the device goes off. Rescuers end up having to pull the baby out, and then they have to pull him out of the car too.

Dr. Robert Montgomery returns to Hopkins after three years and hopes he will be able to operate again. "And due to the kindness of others, they actually allow me to go into the electrophysiology lab with all the equipment that we use in the operating room, and we test all the devices while they monitor my defibrillator, and it doesn't interfere with any of them. I am finally given a green light."

He is allowed to once again practice surgery. He manages not to have any cardiac arrests in the hospital. The only way he can stay a surgeon is to control his heart rhythms. Every stressful situation he goes into, he goes through this sequence of controlling his thoughts, controlling his body's reaction to things. He's able to completely change his outlook. He doesn't go through any formal program for relaxation or mind/body control. He just knows his life depends on not having any sudden stress hormone surges. No fight-or-flight reactions that can set off his defibrillator.

Bob also prays regularly and describes himself as a very spiritual and religious person. He makes peace with his own mortality. He tells me that his father helped guide him before he died and spoke to his son about how faith helped him face his own death. Robert Montgomery, MD, lives with that same philosophy every day.

مليّ

I AM SITTING in Dr. Robert Montgomery's office as he tells me this. His manner is congenial, understated, humble even, though he is one of the top kidney transplant surgeons in the world and the foremost pioneer in xenotransplantation (organ transplants from one species to another). His long hair and long handlebar mustache that extends down below his chin don't fit the classic image I have in my mind of a surgeon. On the other hand, they do fit the look I expect of someone who has come so close to death so many times and has lived to defy it.

He tells me he lives one day at a time. He has had many near-death, out-of-body experiences, where he is comatose following a cardiac arrest and finds himself looking down at the world, not knowing if he will be returning to his body. He has come back from seven cardiac arrests. These near-death experiences heavily impact him and inform his deep faith.

"I've had seven cardiac arrests. And every time it's the same thing. Just actual darkness. And I am not aware until I am coming back into my body and my heart is restarted. In these experiences, I feel a connection to a vastness, a connection to something much bigger than my experiences on earth. I start becoming aware of my own breath, and at first, I'm not sure what the sound is. And just before the moment when all my thoughts and memories are coming back, I am conscious of transcendence that's way beyond anything that's human or of this planet Earth we are on. I feel calm and serene. I feel my soul right before I am in my body. As I am waking up there is this overlap of awareness of this vastness and then knowing that I am a living being. The experience is exactly the same each time."

Dr. Montgomery says this experience helps him to be at peace with who he is, and has enabled him to be a far more effective doctor and surgeon. "I no longer focus on how others view me. I don't hear that. I become more comfortable in my own skin. I'm not inhibited by my own thoughts. I try to connect with people directly in a human way without any intermediaries."

ﻬ

DR. MONTGOMERY LEANS back in his chair in his modest office just behind the operating room suites, clasping his hands together. He recalls his most powerful near-death experience in 2017, when he was working at NYU Langone Health as the head of the transplant service, which began a cascade of events that led to his heart transplant. This is the greatest challenge he has ever faced.

He is in Patagonia with the youngest and oldest of his four children. They are enjoying a rigorous trip of hiking, hunting, and fishing. (His office walls are lined with photos of these remote excursions.) Bob develops a cough that ends up being due to a multidrug-resistant pseudomonas bacteria. It's likely he caught it in the hospital here before the trip, rather than down there.

He finds he can't get out of bed; he has shaking chills; his son says he looks terrible. He's developing sepsis. He sits in the chair and goes into cardiac arrest. Somehow it doesn't hit the threshold for the defibrillator to go off. His son does CPR on him, saving him. This really shakes his son up, but they throw him in the back of a truck and the guide drives them to a tiny hospital in San Martín.

By this time he's in a coma, and the hospital knows they can't handle this. They put him in an ambulance and send him to another town. This is a really remote part of Patagonia. The ICU is tiny and there are only four total patients. While Bob is in there, the other three die.

The lung transplant pulmonologist at NYU, Dr. Luis Angel, flies down. No one thinks Robert Montgomery is likely to survive. He is not getting better in part because they don't realize how resistant the pseudomonas is. His lungs are terrible, filled with secretions, he has necrosis on the back of his scalp, and his feet dangle off the too-short bed, which is really more of a stretcher. Luis says he can't believe the ventilator is working at all; it is so old.

When they finally get him off the ventilator, he can't talk. With no nutrition for over a month, he has lost a tremendous amount of weight. He can't perform tasks or do much of anything. He is like a baby.

Dr. Montgomery fidgets in his chair with the memory.

"But the most fascinating thing that keeps me going the whole time I am in a coma is that I have this entire existence, this life, different from my real life. I am a surgeon at the turn of the twentieth century, in the days when anesthesia is just being invented. I remember all the operations I do. I go to work every day. I use ether to put people to sleep and I boil my instruments to sterilize them. So, while I am in this coma, I am living another sort of existence.

"The experience is so detailed and it seems as if it stretches over the whole time I am in the coma. I remember the days of going to this Victorian hospital on this hill and doing surgery all the time on children and everything. We use ether drops to put them to sleep. But I am not a student of this period of history. I don't have knowledge of it and yet the detail is incredible. This is the clue that it is absolutely real. It can't be from a memory because I lack the memory.

"All I know about the period of time I am living in are based on some pictures I have on my wall of the surgeon William Stewart Halsted, a hero of mine. I'm convinced that living this alternate life at the turn of the century helps me to recover, one of the hardest things I've ever had to do. I wake up after a month. They fly me up to my own hospital, NYU. The rehabilitation is fierce and challenging afterward. Somehow I shake it all off and go back to work, to 'doing my thing.' Which is performing kidney transplants."

Over the next year, Bob Montgomery suffers a series of cardiac arrests, one after another. At a Broadway show, he has to have about forty minutes of CPR when the defibrillator fails. At a convention in Matera, Italy, at four in the morning, at an old hotel with stone floors, he hits the floor and splits his head open. Blood is everywhere. Another time his heart goes into a ventricular tachycardia (rapid heart arrhythmia) storm, and he has one cardiac arrest after another. Four over a three-hour period.

After hitting his head on the stone floor in Matera, an ambulance is called and Bob is brought to the hospital. "In the small hospital in Matera, it seems like Patagonia all over again. A Catholic priest gives me last rites. Believe it or not, I don't get scared or have a fear of dying. I haven't had that for a very long time. I take things as they come. I'm just doing the work of recovering from these things and am happy that I'm still here. That I get another day.

"With my wife's help I sign out of the hospital against medical advice with my IV still in and board a commercial flight back to New York. I am admitted to the NYU intensive care unit and receive a heart transplant three weeks later."

᠁

THE TRANSPLANT INSTITUTE that Dr. Montgomery started at NYU Langone Health in 2016 included heart transplants for the first time. At the same time, Dr. Montgomery helped pioneer the use of donors at risk for transmitting treatable viruses like HIV and hepatitis C, not knowing that he would later receive a heart from just such a hepatitis C donor.

Back when he was at Johns Hopkins, Dr. Montgomery

helped popularize new ways to detect these viruses and use post-transplant antiviral treatment to ensure that the risk of transmission was minimal, or to quickly treat any transmission that did occur. As the opioid crisis hit, there were more hep C–positive donors since intravenous drug use may also transmit hep C. Almost 50,000 die from drug overdoses in 2018, so there is an abundance of hep C organs, and most of them are being discarded.

In 2018, Bob Montgomery accepts a hep-C heart from a donor who overdosed on heroin. Bob becomes infected with hep C, which is then eliminated from his body after two months with antiviral drugs.

"I brought this protocol for treating hepatitis C in transplant patients here to NYU," he says. "We have only used it on a handful of patients by 2018, but I decide I want to be one of them, to show everyone it is safe. I decide to get a hep-C heart from a drug overdose victim."

Dr. Montgomery had recruited the heart transplant surgeon Dr. Nader Moazami to NYU the year before from the Cleveland Clinic.

The surgery goes well, and Bob recovers and goes back to work, building out his transplant program and going on to become NYU Langone Health's chief of surgery in 2023. In this role he is driven by the realization that he has "more work to do." He shifts his sights to xenotransplantation (pig organs). "I think there's something I need to contribute. I think it's xenotransplantation. I think it's a way to solve the organ shortage problem, which is our biggest problem in transplantation."

Fighting the organ shortage has been an important goal throughout Dr. Montgomery's career. There are 100,000 people on the national transplant list yearly, and only a fifth of them receive organs.

Dr. Montgomery has attacked this problem head-on, first with a lottery system for kidney transplants to match donors with recipients, then by championing the use of hepatitis-C hearts while developing a safe protocol for use, and finally by accepting one himself.

IN 2021, DR. Montgomery turns to pig organ transplant, bringing to bear his own training in immunology and the thymus from those years at Oxford to not only guide the operations but to determine the genetic modulation methods and help avoid organ rejection as well. He experiments with implanting a pig thymus in addition to the kidney. By 2024, he has been involved with six xenotransplants.

"We've learned a tremendous amount from all of these six xenotransplants that we've done," he says. "I think it's the solution. I think we need to do clinical trials. And include patients who have a higher likelihood of being able to tolerate it than the ones we're doing now, which are kind of Hail Marys."

The first gene-edited pig-to-human organ transplant takes place at NYU Langone Health in September 2021, in a neurologically deceased person with a beating heart. A pig thymus is also included and is used again in a similar procedure in November 2021, with Dr. Montgomery again operating. In 2022, Dr. Moazami and others perform two gene-edited heart transplants, and in 2023, a sixty-one-day study of a gene-edited pig kidney xenotransplant in a recently deceased man shows optimal performance.

In April 2024, a fifty-four-year-old woman with heart and kidney failure who can no longer tolerate dialysis with a bad heart receives a heart pump (left ventricular assist device, or LVAD) as well as a genetically edited pig kidney and thymus. This is a giant step forward, though unfortunately her heart still gives out. She lives with the organ for forty-seven days.

"We take the kidney out electively," Dr. Montgomery says to me, "because the LVAD is just not able to provide quite enough consistent blood flow to the kidney. It isn't rejected. Whenever she has a problem with her blood pressure, the kidney temporarily doesn't get enough oxygen, which causes damage. I think we've learned a tremendous amount from all six of these xenotransplants that we've done. And I think it's a solution to the shortage of organs."

Dr. Robert Montgomery rises from his chair and gives me a warm handshake. I know that I am in the presence of greatness, but his manner is unassuming, and I know this is a reflection of all he has been through, approaching one day at a time, humble in the face of God.

Bob is also fearless, living each day without knowing if there will be another. He has survived many medical miracles, with more to come. He travels back and forth to Ukraine, performing lifesaving surgeries and delivering surgical equipment and medical supplies. He is a man of deep faith, and his soft yet calloused hands are truly the hands of God.

᷎

THE SEVENTH XENOTRANSPLANT at NYU Langone Health, thirteenth overall, takes place at the end of November 2024, with a genetically altered pig kidney. This one has the potential to be a game changer, as the recipient walks out of the hospital just days after the operation. Dr. Montgomery operates with the help of Dr. Jayme Locke, an all-star transplant surgeon whom Dr. Montgomery has trained. Of the thirteen xenotransplants, this is the fourth involving a living recipient. Her name is Towana Looney, and she is fifty-three years old at the time of the operation. "I'm from a country town in Alabama," she says at a press conference in mid-December at NYU. "I am overjoyed. I'm blessed to have received this gift. A second chance at life . . . I want to give courage to those out there on dialysis."

Towana's story is remarkable, a medical miracle in its own right. She gave one of her own kidneys to her mother in 1999, but due to a rare complication following pregnancy, she ended up on dialysis herself. She badly needed a transplant. As a prior donor, she was put at the top of the list, but there was no compatible donor for her. Not until Dr. Montgomery offered her a different option.

Dr. Montgomery and I meet after the press conference for another sit-down interview, this time in a conference room overlooking the shimmering East River. I ask him just how special he thinks Towana is. "First," he tells me, "she is a hero for being a living donor herself. She gave the gift of life to her mother and then, unfortunately, developed complications from pregnancy, preeclampsia, high blood pressure, blood transfusions, and her remaining kidney failed. So she's someone who already paid a really significant price for an incredible act of generosity. Now she finds herself in a situation where we can't find a match. She's just languishing on dialysis year after year. She is looking for any other possibility, any other chance at having a normal life again. And I think she's going to change the face of transplantation. She's one of those pioneers."

Towana's new kidney lasts for over four months. It is removed on April 4, 2025, when her body rejects it because she had to reduce her antirejection medication due to an infection. Afterward, the courageous patient resumes dialysis.

As the recipient of a heart transplant himself, Dr. Montgomery is a staunch advocate for others in similar straits and he is constantly pushing for solutions to the profound shortage of body organs.

He says to me, "Less than one percent of the people who die every year, far less, die in a way where they could be a donor. At the same time, the number of people who could benefit from an organ transplant continues to increase. And so my epiphany in living through that myself (and realizing that I probably wouldn't live through it) and making it to getting an organ was that we needed another source of organs. It's either going to be pig organs or organs that are manufactured in the lab. I think the bioartificial organs are

THE MIRACLES AMONG US

much further away, and xenotransplantation or pig organs are what's in front of us right now."

Dr. Montgomery tells me that with the number of human kidneys transplanted remaining at 5,000 to 6,000 per year for the past fifteen years, while over the same time the demand has continued to increase, xenotransplantation with pig organs is the game changer we need. "It's something that's renewable, and it's sustainable," he says, smiling.

CHAPTER 13

Dan the Man

I HAVE KNOWN CARDINAL TIMOTHY DOLAN, the tenth and current archbishop of New York, for many years. I have run into him, among other places, in the greenroom at *Fox & Friends*, waiting to go on TV: the cardinal there to espouse spiritual healing, and me to espouse physical healing. Whenever I speak to him, I am reminded of the central role faith plays in *all* healing.

When we speak in an interview, Dolan sets out his views, which, as they often do, set him apart from the strictest church interpretations. "I highly appreciate what I call 'soft miracles,'" he says. "The convergence of providence and health care. Isn't it beautiful the way things sometimes turn out? We never exclude the participants in the miracle. Take the case of my sister Lisa. Her daughter has bone cancer. She is surviving against all odds. We pray for her."

"How is she doing?" I ask.

"So far so good," the cardinal says. "She thanks God, chemo, surgery, and her daughter's doctor, Dr. Bergamini.

Lisa says, 'Yes, I believe in prayer.' Bergamini is one of the ways God answers my prayers. She says, 'God saves my daughter, and so does Bergamini.'"

"We seek the exceptional," Cardinal Dolan says. "We believe in miracles, where the outcome goes beyond the predicted. These miracles are rare. When my niece is very sick with cancer, she goes to what they call the Lourdes of Ireland, County of Mayo—the shrine of Saint Valentine, Dublin, Ireland. Our Lady of Lourdes Shrine. My niece says, 'I am very much at peace; either the Lord will answer me and cure me, or I will end up in His arms.'"

Cardinal Dolan tells me that we must trust in God's grace and trust in divine intervention. "The Lord works a miracle here," he says, "but why not more often? This is what leads to doubters. Why some and not others? Why not me?"

He tells me that God answers all prayers, but we don't know how, when, or why. One of his parishioners, Bob Schwagel, had diabetes and lost his sight and went to Lourdes to pray, but he never got his sight back. He grew very depressed and was put in a psych ward. He prayed to God, "Heal me or take me home." He fell and gashed his leg and died. His prayer was actually answered. His sight wasn't restored but the Lord took him home. In the rearview mirror, the Lord answered.

"More often miracles are subtle," Dolan says. "They come to us in breezes, not in thunder and lightning. We never want to go to snake handlers, or mystics like the golden calf story in the Old Testament. Instead, we combine the contemporary, the holistic, and the role of faith. Choreography blends it all together. Scientific advances together with the power of faith and prayer. The spiritual with the physical."

Dolan talks to me about St. Padre Pio, a twentieth-century priest known for his work with the poor and his great piety and humility. "He endorsed the physical approach," Dolan says. "He was an agent of healing. He would blush and run the other way. He was witness to many miracles of secondary causality, meaning that the miracle has an associated medical explanation. As opposed to the very rare miracles where no natural explanation exists, where attestation is required by medical professionals to ascertain a Church-recognized miracle. Pio became famous for his spiritual and physical fights against the devil and demons." Dolan says that miracles of secondary causality (soft miracles) are also based on the philosophy of St. Thomas Aquinas, where both reason and faith are necessary, where other people, other agents are needed to bring out God's will. Dolan says that people also routinely pray to St. Anthony of Padua, called the "miracle worker," that the Lord will heal them, and that they will profit spiritually from bodily ills. One prayer to St. Anthony for the sick includes this plea: "Help me, then, good St. Anthony, in sickness and trouble. Teach me, please, how to profit spiritually from my bodily ills. Intercede for me with God so that my health may improve. When recovered in body, let me be also improved in spirit, too."

Cardinal Dolan says the complete lack of a natural explanation is rare, and not necessary for a "soft miracle." These so-called soft miracles are the main miracles of this book. "We can't sit in judgment of how and when God's miracles occur,"

Cardinal Dolan says. "Whether a physician is a believer or not, he is a participant of the transcendent. The tools and ingredients within the physician are there to solve the problem. The resilience of the human body and spirit helps and combines with prayer to overcome and transcend.

"Miracles of healing," Cardinal Dolan says, "are evidence of God's grace. Physicians have the hands of God. The human body is healable. The balance can be restored. We can intervene and remove something toxic. Doctors and patients learn to trust in the nature of the human body, and that there is something beyond us (the divine) in which we can trust."

Faith combines with great doctoring to aid outcomes. Roughly 77 percent of American adults affiliate with some organized religious group, according to the 2020 Census of American Religion, and utilize their faith to help them get through disasters and cope with devastating illnesses.

❧

DR. ROBERT REDFIELD, former director of the Centers for Disease Control and Prevention (CDC), knows Cardinal Dolan, having worked with him during the humanitarian relief efforts following the 2010 Haiti earthquake. Redfield found Dolan to be extremely wise and centered.

I have known Dr. Redfield since the beginning of the COVID pandemic. I traveled to his house in Maryland in June 2021, after he left the CDC at the conclusion of President Donald Trump's first term in the White House,

I interviewed him for over an hour, was impressed by his wife Joy's generosity, and we stayed in contact afterward. He is soft-spoken and careful with his words, mild-mannered and thoughtful, never attacking or openly criticizing anyone. When Redfield's son Bobby, a renowned kidney transplant surgeon, came to NYU Langone for a job interview, I was part of the team that interviewed him. Like his father, I found Bobby to be warmhearted, easily approachable, and humble despite his prodigious talents.

۔مطہ

ON JANUARY 20, 2023, the Redfield family experiences a great tragedy. Robert and Joy's son Dan Redfield travels down to a resort in the Florida Keys known as Ocean Reef. He is there on a business trip, and he is a passenger in a golf cart driving along the road. According to Dr. Redfield, there have been a number of serious accidents involving these carts.

Dan Redfield falls out of the golf cart and likely hits his head on something, according to emergency responders. It is clear he is seriously injured. "There is reportedly blood coming out of his mouth," Dr. Redfield Sr. tells me. "He isn't conscious. When the ambulance group comes, they immediately call the helicopter and the ER and bring him to Jackson South Trauma."

At the trauma center at Jackson South at the University of Miami, Dan Redfield is seen initially by Dr. Enrique Ginsberg.

When Dan reaches Jackson, he is minimally responsive, with one eye pupil that is fixed and dilated. His Glasgow Coma Scale at the time isn't known. Multiple studies have shown that trauma patients with two "blown pupils" and a Glasgow Coma Scale of 3 have very little chance of long-term survival. A blown pupil refers to a pupil that doesn't respond or react to light being shown into the patient's eyes, an indication that the brain is herniating out of the skull. The Glasgow Coma Scale is a way of assessing responsiveness on hospital admission following head trauma. Three is the lowest score and corresponds to zero responsiveness, and 15 is the highest, which indicates the patient is fully responsive. According to research, "Patients with head injury with low Glasgow Coma Scale (GCS) scores on hospital admission have a poor prognosis. A GCS score of 3 is the lowest possible score and is associated with an extremely high mortality rate, with some researchers suggesting that there is no chance of survival."

According to Dr. Redfield, Dan quickly responds to mannitol, an osmotic diuretic that decreases swelling in tissues, and his blown pupil once again responds and reacts. This is seen as a more positive sign.

Studies have shown that there is more than a 40 percent survival rate if the eye pupil returns to normal size and function within the first two hours, which Dan's does, and that many trauma patients do respond to therapy with the diuretic mannitol, which decreases intracranial pressures.

Redfield tells me that a young intern at the hospital named Connor is the one who alertly gives his son mannitol and then wheels him up to the OR, where the neurosurgeons at first think he isn't salvageable and they aren't planning to operate. "Well, Connor, when the pupil comes back, says to them, 'Hey, the pupil came back.' So, within thirty-five minutes, they have him in the OR. Within thirty-five minutes of the helicopter landing, he is having his skull removed to relieve the pressure."

Removing the skull allows the swollen brain to expand. Otherwise, the pressure and compression within the skull will lead to more and more tissue damage. Studies show that decompressing the brain in this fashion can improve outcomes dramatically.

Dr. Redfield becomes very emotional recalling what has happened to his son, whom he loves so much. "They remove his skull, and they literally remove it in multiple pieces. So pretty much from the top of his forehead. You know, three-quarters of the way back, all of that skull bone is gone. And, of course, his brain now can move up and out of the confinement. Joy and I get down to the hospital along with Danny's wife, Lindsay, and we are basically told to prepare for the reality that Danny isn't going to make it. That they feel that his neurological assessment at the time he gets into their hospital is not compatible with survival. And then they remove the top of the skull. He's intubated, on the ventilator. He's got a jillion different tubes and lines and an intracranial hemorrhage. Bleeding in all the lobes of the brain. If you look at his CT scans, the brain is so traumatized. His brain stem, which controls so many basic functions, is extremely swollen."

"Danny's recovery is nothing short of miraculous in my mind," his brother, the transplant surgeon Dr. Robert Redfield III, says to me in an interview. "His initial scan shows a tremendous amount of frontal and significant amount of temporal damage to the brain. Even more concerning is the amount of edema [swelling] he has in his brain stem, where so many basic functions are performed. And that's what I am most worried about as a surgeon. It's very hard to decompress all that. I think most people would say this is a nonsurvivable injury. I think my dad gets a lot of credit for how aggressive he is, you know; he has some balls rolling, his connections, and he pushes, and they do a hemicraniectomy, which is a pretty aggressive move where they took off the front half of his skull emergently, and allow his brain to swell. But I am still really worried about the brain stem and the cerebellar injuries. We are all very, very worried about that because there's not really a good decompression option for the lower part of the brain.

"So, I think the removal of a big part of his skull allows him to live and survive. Most people I speak to really feel he is going to be a vegetable for the rest of his life."

Over the next several days, as Redfield and his wife, Joy, pray, their son is given steroids to further reduce the brain swelling and he is kept mostly in a supine position. Dr. Redfield Sr. says, "They can't sit him up for over ten days because his brain stem would get too swollen and then his heart rate would go nuts, his temperature would go nuts. They don't think that he will probably survive. His face is swollen. Everything is swollen.

"We pray constantly for him there, you know, and we pray, and we pray," Dr. Redfield Sr. says.

"We hum," Joy Redfield says. "We hum. We don't sing. We hum. At least, I hum. Because we think if we sing, he might be singing. You see the pearly gates. So instead, I hum."

"We get him anointed by a priest, Father Daniel," Dr. Redfield Sr. says. "We are told to expect that he will never wake up."

But still, the Redfields refuse to give up. "I feel that the best trauma center in the world is the shock unit at the University of Maryland up in Baltimore," Redfield the father tells me. "I ask the head doctor there, Tom Scalea, who I know well, about getting him transferred up to shock trauma when he is stable enough."

They end up renting a plane with a medical team to air-evac Danny to shock trauma in Maryland. He is comatose on a ventilator. They bring multiple supplies, multiple tubes. Bobby—his brother the trauma surgeon—goes with them to bring him up to Maryland.

"He has a bad brain injury," Scalea tells me in an interview. Peering at Scalea's worn, grizzled features over Zoom, gray-haired with deeply recessed dark eyes, I decide he has the look of either the careful experienced surgeon he is or a fishing boat captain who is so seasoned that he is the only one with the wherewithal and wisdom to bring you back in from a sudden ferocious storm before you capsize.

"You can come all the way back from this. It happens," Scalea says. "It's not fifty percent, it's not twenty-five percent, not even ten percent, much less. It depends on the degree of underlying trauma and on the amount of direct injury to the brain. The prognosis is worse if you have a huge amount of direct injury."

Scalea recalls seeing a lot of edema in Danny's brain on the early CT scans. Scalea says that taking the skull off in Miami and allowing the brain to decompress is lifesaving by allowing the intracranial pressure to go down.

After that, Scalea says, comes a long waiting game. "There's no real pharmacologic therapy for brain injury. The real therapy for brain injury is to take care of the rest of the body. What we're trying to do is make a cocoon in which an injured brain can live while it recovers. So, you know, it's a matter of oxygenation and ventilation and cerebral blood flow and nutrition and avoiding fever and treating infection. But once the brain is decompressed and the pressure is relieved, then there's not a lot of direct treatment for the brain injury."

Scalea is proud of his trauma center and how they elevate their treatments to high art and create medical miracles with their work. "We are the only dedicated trauma hospital in the United States," he says. "And I think when you do it sixty-five hundred, seventy-five hundred times a year, you develop a real sensitivity for the nuances of terrible injury. And that allows us to pick up things maybe earlier than they would be picked up elsewhere. I give most of the credit for that to the nurses who are there at the bedside. But this is what we do. It's all we do. And so, there's no mission creep here. This is an entire institution dedicated to the care of the badly injured patient. And I just think that this many times a year allows us to do things that just don't get done very often elsewhere at the level we're able to do them. I think that's fair.

"Here's one example. We took care of a sixteen-year-old young girl with an awful brain injury a number of years ago. And she ended up with multiple organ failure. She was on very high-driving-pressure ventilation, and we opened her abdomen. We decompressed her abdomen to help with her lungs expanding and decrease her intracranial [brain] pressure. And we stood her straight up on a tilt table to try to lower the pressure on her brain. And we still couldn't succeed. I put her on ECMO [reoxygenating the blood] to treat her respiratory failure in order to drop her intracranial pressure. Nobody else would have done that. In order to do this, in order to get the catheter into her jugular vein for the ECMO, we had to climb up on an actual ladder to do the neck dissection right there in the ICU. So, what does that mean? It means that we're willing to invent seemingly crazy solutions to save a single life. And I think that that's part of the fabric of this place. It is resource-intensive. It is expensive. It is heartbreaking when it doesn't work. But the dedication we have to bring everything we have to a single patient really drives our ability to come up with some of these miracles, these great saves."

This attention to fine detail leads directly to Dan's save, which would have been close to impossible somewhere else. It speaks to Cardinal Dolan's idea of great science being a crucial part of miracle saves. "Whenever we move him, his intracranial pressures would change," Scalea says. "So, he is very tenuous for a number of days. But we are very aggressive about nutrition and getting people out of bed. Dan is very, very sick. If you are going to bet on him making as good a recovery as he does, everybody would say it's extremely unlikely. And yet he has a spectacular result."

Three weeks after arriving at Maryland Shock Trauma, Dan begins to make substantial neurological progress. Scalea explains to me that people with bad brain injuries tend to wake up "over a prolonged period of time." Scalea says he has known Bob Redfield Sr. for twenty-five years. They went to Haiti together after the earthquake in 2010, at a time when Redfield also worked with Cardinal Dolan. Scalea acknowledges that the former CDC director is deeply religious and that this plays a role in his son's amazing recovery, though they disagree on how much.

Scalea says that it is clear that Dan hit his head, causing the initial injury, and that the extent of the injury is substantial. He says that his initial score at Jackson South on the Glasgow Coma Scale is low, but that this scale alone isn't the only predictor in terms of long-term outcome at Shock Trauma. Scalea says he has been a trauma surgeon for forty years and has been in charge at Maryland Shock Trauma for twenty-seven years. *Vegetative state*, he says, is a term he doesn't use; he always gives a patient a chance for recovery and does his best to bring them there. Miracles at his hospital aren't passive; they are the result of consistent hard work, expertise, and never giving up.

I ask Dr. Bobby Redfield, Danny's brother, how a full recovery is even possible with all the swelling and damage.

"They allow the brain to swell. And most people would just say it's not even worth it. You know, it's not going to be survivable injuries. So why take half his skull off, and why keep him in the hospital for so many weeks? Tracheotomy, feeding tube, all those things. And, yeah, I mean, he has extraordinary care, aggressive care. You know, I do think the reason he survives is because of a lot of aggressive medical actions, which come all together and pay off. No one thinks he will be back driving a car or that a year after the accident you will be able to have a conversation with him. No one would predict that he would return to a way of living that is not much different than before, where he can take care of himself. Like, if you talk to him, you wouldn't know anything was up. Danny's injury and the whole process of his recovery makes me rediscover my faith. And I really was a typical kind of scientist. I liked the tradition of Catholicism but not the faith, but Danny's injury and his miraculous recovery really convert me back to religion. There is no other explanation for what happens."

When I talk to Scalea, I recognize that I am in the presence of greatness, consummate skill and confidence, vast experience, and the most essential ingredient of all, ice water running through his veins. Recovery is a coordinated effort between doctors and nurses there, as they do everything they can to keep the pressures in the brain as low as possible so the brain can heal. Scalea is methodical: He approaches healing one step at a time, and doesn't pause to marvel at the result.

꙳

"THE ACCIDENT OCCURRED on January twentieth, 2023," Dan's mother, Joy, says, "and then on March first I suddenly feel he is back inside of himself."

"After that, he wakes up gradually," Dr. Redfield Sr. says. "When he awakens, the first thing he wants to do is pray with us. And he can't talk, of course, but he squeezes our hands."

Dan's wife, Lindsay, sits with him for hours, holding his hands and staring into his eyes. She communicates constantly with the staff, who are very attentive to Dan. She never seems to give up hope.

"Scalea is preparing me that even if he does recover," Robert Redfield Sr. says, "he will likely be highly compromised and never fully functional. But Joy and I have a lot of conversations with God, and we do feel in our hearts that he is going to fully recover. My son Bobby, the surgeon, thinks we are crazy at first. He says, 'He's not going to recover, Dad. You know he's going to require thirty to fifty million dollars of care over the next twenty years. And you know we should stop thinking that he's going to fully recover because it won't happen.'"

As Dan starts to wake up, the surgeons aren't able to replace his skull because it is in pieces and unsterile, so they use a 3-D printer to make a titanium skull implant. Dr. Redfield Sr. says, "They have to graft a new membrane to cover the brain and then put the titanium skull back on that. And finally, by the middle of April, he has his titanium skull in and is getting to the point where he can go to their close head injury rehab program too. And he spends another four to six weeks in rehab. They have to teach him how to walk again. We still feel in our hearts that he is going to completely recover."

Rehabilitation plays a huge role with Dan and with all brain trauma patients. "And getting people out to rehab as early as possible is really important," Scalea says. Dan makes it to rehab in three to four weeks, crucial to his recovery.

"We just don't give up. We just don't," Scalea says matter-of-factly. "Dan has a terrible injury and is quite ill when he gets to Jackson South, and if you ask me what's the average result from that, well, it isn't anything like what we get with Dan Redfield. Is this a spectacular result to have somebody that's this sick? Who is obtunded [comatose] for a long time? The answer is yes. Should someone in this condition make a complete neurologic recovery? The answer is, very, very rarely. He is close to the person he was before he got hurt. He may have little bits of deficit, but if you meet him for the first time, you would have no idea of what happened to him. A miracle by anyone's definition."

"While he is in rehab," Dr. Redfield Sr. says, "we meet in the cafeteria and I look at my son, and I see that one of his eyes is focused in one direction and the other one is focused on me. And I say, 'Danny, you see double, don't you?' You know, I guess that's bothersome. And he says, 'No, Dad, I don't see double.' And I say, 'What? What do you mean?' He says, 'Well, I'm blind in my right eye. I can't see anything in my right eye.'

"Joy and I don't say anything to Danny. We talk to God. We say, 'We feel You planted in our hearts that Danny is going to have a complete recovery. And we don't consider being blind in the right eye complete recovery.'"

"You criticize God?" I ask him.

"Why not? It works. Two to three weeks later Danny has perfect vision in both eyes."

"Another miracle."

DR. ROBERT REDFIELD Sr. has had a long association with the Catholic Church that goes back decades to his early battles against HIV/AIDS in the 1980s. When Dan Redfield first becomes comatose, his father turns to a group of Franciscan sisters he is close to in Peekskill, New York. Sister Antonia McGuire is in charge. She started a ministry decades before for men who were dying of AIDS, and now she sings prayers for Danny's recovery that "go all the way through the church, all the way through the bishop's choir. They even make their way up to Pope Francis, who begins praying for Danny's recovery."

Dr. Redfield puts a crucifix around his son's neck during his recovery. He firmly believes that God isn't finished with his son yet, and that it is God's will that he lives. "Our first son, John Paul, died," Redfield tells me. "We prayed, and he died. It was God's will. I don't know why God chooses to save Danny, but He does. Danny's recovery is not fully consistent with medical knowledge. Danny, if he does recover, is much more likely to have significant impairments."

Instead of giving in to these seemingly inevitable impairments, Redfield says, he imagines the day when his son will be back out there playing golf at the same high level as before the accident. He hopes and prays that he will reach the point of having to just reteach himself how to swing a golf club.

"I've been part of miracle investigations," Dr. Redfield tells me. "I was part of Pope John Paul's delegation for the World Day for the Sick in 1992 to Lourdes. I was the only nonordained individual in the delegation. I flew on the Vatican plane with all the cardinals, and I spent five days there. I was allowed to sit in on the investigation of the miracle. They take the science very seriously, and not all who vote on miracles are observant."

During a conference on AIDS with Pope John Paul II back in the 1980s, Dr. Redfield was tapped to meet the pontiff, who taught him three lessons that he was later able to apply to his son's illness. The first lesson is not to see God as just an energy force, that doing good things in the world and displaying good energy is the path to heaven. The pope told Redfield that you need to build a personal relationship with God. The second lesson is that prayer is the most powerful tool we have, and that we need to learn how to use it. The third lesson is that there is redemptive value in human suffering. Dr. Redfield pushed back against the pope, saying that as a doctor he saw no value in suffering. But during that trip to Lourdes he changed his mind and saw that the pope was right. He came back to the US and tried to apply this lesson to his patients with AIDS. "Most of my patients were young men and women in the prime of their life. They were dying and they were suffering. And I tried to empower them to harvest the redemptive value of human suffering. One of the ways I did it, particularly the men who were in their thirties and forties, who had families they had left because they discovered that they were gay and went off with a male partner—I was able to reunify those families, at least emotionally reunify them before the husband died, or the wife died. They found with surprise they were accepted back. Cardinal O'Connor also tried to teach me this in New York when we were working at St. Clare's Hospital—you remember the hospital that took care of so many AIDS patients in New York. He used to tell me that there was redemptive value in human suffering and that people with open hearts would embrace you. And I used to tell him I don't buy it. I now know he is right. Pope John Paul II and Cardinal O'Connor helped me to learn."

When it comes to his son, Dr. Redfield says, "We never feel alone. We never feel desperate. We always have confidence that God is going to walk with us through this challenge, independent of how it ends up. We have lost one child already. And our other son, Bobby, who says at first we are not in the real world, ends up understanding that Danny's survival and clinical course is directly influenced by God. He sees the miracle."

Joy Redfield is not always as confident. "We are hanging like a little kitty-cat off the church," she says. "I see the church as an ark, and I see us on the string hanging there, trying to keep our head above water. Hanging on for dear life."

ه‍ل

AS SOMEONE WITH trauma training himself, Dr. Bobby
Redfield III is completely blown away by how his brother
comes all the way back from being completely unresponsive
to what he is now able to do. "He's able to take care of his
life. He's able to play golf. He's able to hang out with his
kids, drive himself, and be completely independent, and he
just came up on his year anniversary where, I mean, both
bilateral frontal lobes of his brain were practically obliterated. One of his temporal lobes was significantly injured. His
cerebellum was out and his brain stem. It's unbelievable. I
mean, the best case we were looking at was he was going to
be hospital bedbound with a trach peg [to breathe through]
in a nursing home. Basically, in a vegetative state. That was
best best-case scenario. Best case. Wow."

I ask Bobby if he can pinpoint the moment when his
brother turns a corner toward recovery. He says that six weeks
after the accident, his brother still isn't doing anything. He
still thinks he is finished. He tells me they've taken all the
sedation out. His head is sunken in. He isn't responding. "I
am getting really agitated because my parents are still holding on to hope, and my dad is like, 'I think it's going to
be fine.' He says we just need to pray harder. And I walk
in, and he's got, you know, Mother Teresa's crucifix on his
chest, and even the hospital staff is like, these people—your
parents—are a little out of touch with reality right now. And
I agree that I don't see a path forward." Bobby pauses, a calm
surgeon whose voice suddenly trembles with emotion. "And

so, then a couple of weeks after that, my sister Patty calls me and says, 'You wouldn't believe it, but I was just in his room. And he started following commands.' So then he nods his head and squeezes my sister's hand, and she says, 'Hey, Dan, if you can hear me, I'm just going to play some of your favorite music.' And Dan is big into musicals. And he loves *Les Mis*. She shows him a list of songs from musicals, and when she reaches one of his favorites from *Les Mis*, he squeezes her hand. It is clear he wants to hear it. And so, from this moment on, I know his personality has survived. He is there. And this is an amazing event. Then it is a pretty rapid recovery after this. He gets to rehab. He is in a wheelchair."

Bobby sighs. "I mean, his soul has left and come back. He was basically dead on arrival at the hospital."

☙

THESE DAYS, DAN is traveling around the country, golfing the best courses in different states, and performing quite well. He has overcome basic fundamental problems, from learning to walk the stairs to brushing his teeth again. The months leading up to the accident and for many months after are a blur. He remembers taking the kids trick-or-treating for Halloween but doesn't remember Christmas or New Year's prior to the accident. He doesn't recognize Shock Trauma when he revisits it, and at first he doesn't recognize his house or his family. His short-term memory doesn't exist; his long-term memory comes back slowly. He needs to relearn that these are his shoes, his hat, his country club. He has to relearn his golf driver and five-iron. He has to reacquaint himself with the fact that he has worked for Congress for ten years.

Through it all, his wife, Lindsay, remains completely devoted to his care and his recovery. She stays by his side and helps him to remember and return to his life. She has been patient and loving throughout, never wavering in her devotion or commitment to his full recovery. Now she participates in his joy at his regained freedom, where every day is a gift from God.

In May 2024, Dan is brought back to the room where he was for more than a month. A medical tower with tubes, trachs, IVs. He remembers nothing. Photos seem to be showing someone else. He fails to recognize himself. Someone who was there for some reason. But when someone who is shot (appears to be dead) at an Orioles game and is brought to the roof of Shock Trauma and survives thanks to the great team there, it helps to jog Dan's memory.

There is a picture of Dan on a stretcher with seventeen doctors surrounding him from different disciplines. Doctors who can tell why a patient is there, what's injured, and what needs to be treated right away. Skull, thigh, calf muscle. Ninety percent of patients with Dan's injuries die, the doctors all say. Absolutely none of the 10 percent come all the way back.

It is clear to every member of the Redfield family that Danny's life is not meant to be over there at Shock Trauma. Now Dan is playing the top golf course in every state in the country. His family joins him joyfully and then returns home; he will follow soon. He still scores in the low 80s despite all that he has been through.

ᵱ

FROM THE POINT of view of this book, it doesn't matter whether you view Danny's recovery as a miracle due to tremendous doctoring and trauma nursing and rehab care, the very best in the country, or you invoke divine intervention to be able to fathom it. It may be one or the other or a combination, which is the way I see it and the way Cardinal Dolan sees it. You can choose between Scalea's more grounded scientific view and Robert Redfield Sr.'s more faith-based perspective (the two have had frequent debates over this exact question). But no matter how you view it, Dan Redfield's next birdie on the golf course is a testament to the power of survival, the power of love, of science, and of God.

HEALING
PRAYERS

Dear God and Father of us all,

You are the Lord of healing and wholeness. You have told us You are closest to us when we are suffering or sick. You sent Your Son, Jesus, as the Divine Physician, and He restored sight, hearing, life itself, bringing us to the fullness of health You desire for us. His mother, Mary, and His angels and saints intercede for us when we are sick, and Your doctors and nurses are agents of Your grace. Thus, dear Lord, do we trust in You, who lives and reigns forever! Amen.

TIMOTHY MICHAEL DOLAN,
ARCHBISHOP OF NEW YORK

We varied our healing prayers,
but always ended with:

"Thank You, Lord, for all of our blessings.
Please help Paul to heal fully and to
get home soon to live a normal life.
We are one day closer.
In Your name, Amen."

———————————————————

BRET BAIER,
FOX NEWS ANCHOR, WHOSE SON, PAUL,
WAS BORN WITH HEART DISEASE

———————————————————

Dear Father God,

You revealed Yourself in Scripture as the Lord God our healer, and I ask You to restore health and strength to me. Give me and the physicians the wisdom and direction we need. I pray that any medications I take will help and not hurt me, and that You will do what doctors cannot do. I ask for Your comfort and grace to walk through this season. My trust is in You, God, my strength and my refuge. Fill me with Your peace that passes all understanding. I look to You as my healer, and I pray this in the name of Jesus. Amen.

SCRIPTURE REFERENCES:
Exodus 15:26, Jeremiah 30:17, James 1:5, Psalm 46:1, Philippians 4:6–7, 2 Corinthians 2:9

LISA OSTEEN COMES,
ASSOCIATE PASTOR OF LAKEWOOD CHURCH,
WHO WAS MIRACULOUSLY CURED FROM
A DEBILITATING CONDITION AT BIRTH

Lord,

You are the God who heals.

There is healing in Your **wings** (Malachi 4:2),

healing in Your **wounds** (Isaiah 53:5),

and healing in Your **Word** (Psalm 107:20).

We receive Your restoration—

body, mind, and spirit.

Let Your presence surround us,

Your Word strengthen us,

and Your glory protect us.

"Then your salvation will come like the dawn,

and your wounds will quickly heal . . ."

—Isaiah 58:8 (NLT)

In Jesus's name, Amen.

SAMUEL RODRIGUEZ,
LEAD PASTOR OF NEW SEASON CHURCH AND
PRESIDENT OF THE NATIONAL HISPANIC
CHRISTIAN LEADERSHIP CONFERENCE

My favorite healing prayer is the Book of Psalms.

Not just one psalm, but the entire Book of Psalms.

I quote my revered father of blessed memory,

Rav Ovadia Yosef, who would say that so long

as one pours their heart out when reading Psalms

and has tears flowing from their eyes,

this is the way to pray for genuine healing.

RABBI DAVID YOSEF,
SEPHARDIC CHIEF RABBI OF ISRAEL

Heavenly Father,

I thank You that through the blood of Jesus I have been delivered from the kingdom of darkness and brought into the Kingdom of light. I ask for Your power to bring life to my mortal body today. Give me Your strength and Your healing. Restore my health. Grant me endurance. Direct my path. You are my Life, my Hope, and my Deliverer.

In Jesus's name, Amen.

ALLEN JACKSON,
PASTOR OF THE
WORLD OUTREACH CHURCH

In the Psalms, King David says, "My tears have been my food day and night, while they say to me all the day long 'Where is your God?'" (Psalm 42:3).
This implies that his greatest pain was the feeling that God was not apparent in the world.

Similarly, in the High Holiday prayers, we say, "Every creation will know its creator." This expresses our greatest prayer and wish: That the world be healthy and filled with the recognition of God in every aspect of existence.

RABBI MANIS FRIEDMAN,
COUNSELOR, LECTURER, AND PHILOSOPHER;
DEAN OF BAIS CHANA WOMEN INTERNATIONAL;
AND AUTHOR OF *DOESN'T ANYONE BLUSH ANYMORE?*

Healing comes from the Divine quality of *tiferet*, the majestic beauty of integration, and God's own *rachamim*, the compassion whose root is in the life-giving power of the womb. May we be blessed with the health that comes from wholeness, may we merit to see all the brokenness of life stitched together into a beautiful reflection of Divine will, and may we be held by God's compassion, all our wounds bound up with His love and our tears wiped away forever, as the prophet said, "And the Lord God shall wipe the tears from every face."(Isaiah 25:8)

RABBI MIKE FEUER,
CREATOR OF THE
JEWISH HEROISM PROJECT

When his sister, Miriam, is stricken with leprosy, Moses prays a short but effective one-line healing prayer: "Please, God, heal her." (Numbers 12:13) Many people still use this line in their prayers for the ill, and I find it very powerful.

RABBI EFREM GOLDBERG,
RABBI OF THE BOCA RATON
SYNAGOGUE

Lord, We humbly come before You seeking healing, trusting in Your unconditional love and unlimited power. We pray the promise of Jeremiah 30:17: "I will restore you to health and heal your wounds."

Lord, surround Your people with supernatural comfort. We pray "You are the God of all comfort." (2 Corinthians 1:3–4)

And Lord, thank You for granting strength, wisdom, and peace to caregivers. We pray that "Your strength is made perfect in our weakness." (2 Corinthians 12:9–11)

REV. DOUG CLAY,
GENERAL SUPERINTENDENT OF THE
ASSEMBLIES OF GOD (USA)

Your Word is life and health to my
whole being. I receive the joy that heals,
the peace that restores, and the abundance
Jesus promised. I boldly declare:
I am completely healed, in Jesus's name.

Amen.

MIKE KAI,
PASTOR OF INSPIRE CHURCH, HAWAII

"He heals the
brokenhearted and
binds up their wounds."
(Psalms 147:3 NIV)

Shannon Bream,
host of *Fox News Sunday*

Prayer of Saint John Chrysostom

4th Century

O Lord, who heals every infirmity
and cures every illness, visit
and heal Your servants,
granting them release from pain
and restoration to health and vigor,
that they may give thanks to You
and bless Your holy name.
For You are our God, the source of
healing and salvation, and to You
we give glory, now and forever.

Amen.

This ancient prayer of St. John Chrysostom means so much to me, and has brought me hope in times of pain.

―――――――――――――――――――――

ROBERT STEARNS,
BISHOP OF THE TABERNACLE CHURCH
AND FOUNDER AND PRESIDENT
OF EAGLES, WINGS"

―――――――――――――――――――――

I wish you all good health

and a long life.

_____

Marc Siegel

_____

CHAPTER 14

Congressman Scalise

ON JUNE 14, 2017, IN the early morning, a gunman walks onto a baseball field at Eugene Simpson Park in Alexandria, Virginia. Republic congressmen are practicing for the charity baseball game with their Democrat counterparts. The next day is the annual Congressional Baseball Game, where members of the two political parties play against each other. It's a tradition going back to 1909, and it raises millions of dollars to support local causes.

They are nearing the end of practice, with plans to head to the House afterward. House Majority Whip Steve Scalise is standing on second base when he hears a loud noise, like a tractor backfiring. When he hears another pop, he knows it's a gun.

The first shot is fired toward Congressman Trent Kelly at third base and only misses him because it happens to hit a link in the fence, a miracle miss. The groundskeeper had locked just the third base gate the night before, almost as if he had a premonition, which now keeps the shooter from the field. So he is shooting from outside the fence rather than just walking right onto the field.

The gunman's second shot hits Scalise in the hip—a single shot from a semiautomatic rifle. He falls down. He never sees the shooter, who is over by the third base dugout. On the ground he can still hear gunfire, so he starts crawling away from the sound. He makes it about twenty feet into the out-field before his arms give out.

Scalise starts praying, just to make it through the day. He can hear an exchange of gunfire as Capitol Police engage with the shooter and ultimately take him down.

Scalise has only been hit once, but the shooter has also hit a lobbyist, an aide, and one of the officers. Somehow he hasn't killed anyone.

As soon as Scalise hears "shooter down," he sees his colleague Congressman Brad Wenstrup. Wenstrup is a doctor and an Iraq War vet. He had considered leaving the prac-tice early, but stayed to get some extra batting practice in. "Thank God he's here to check on me," thinks Scalise.

"My experience in Iraq is always with me," Wenstrup says to me in an interview. "When you actually get in the combat arena, and you're dealing with severe injuries, you are doing it sometimes under gunfire, mortar fire, rocket fire. When you treat the wounded, there's a triage method, and some wounded have to go right into the OR. The suddenness of severe combat casualties is something you don't see in the civilian sector, even at a Level One trauma center. My army training as a surgeon certainly pays off that day at the base-ball field, which has the feel of actual combat."

Wenstrup is very familiar with the protocol that takes over in dealing with someone who has been shot. "If someone bleeds out, they die. And so one of the first things you have to address is whether the bleeding is external or internal and what you can do to try to stop it. If there's external bleeding, you're going to put on compression as best you can. When the bleeding is more internal, you need rapid surgical intervention to stop bleeding. With Scalise, most of the bleeding is internal."

Wenstrup sweeps his back and other areas to see if there are other wounds besides the obvious one on his hip. There aren't any others, thank God, he thinks. He pulls down Scalise's pants, and he can see the entry wound. He can tell entry wounds because they are small, while exit wounds are large. Wenstrup is anticipating severe trauma from an exit wound, but he doesn't find it. He realizes that the bullet has gone through his hip and up into his abdomen, which is very bad. Yet somehow Steve is still conscious. The staffer who has been hit across the chest is visibly bleeding heavily. Everyone on the field assumes he is the priority because they can see his bleeding.

But Wenstrup realizes Steve is the one who is actually dying, because the bullet has torn him up inside.

Worried about the femoral artery, which runs deep in the thigh, Wenstrup puts a belt on his upper leg as a tourniquet. He's also worried about the iliac arteries inside the pelvis. Wenstrup asks Scalise to move his left foot. He can't move it. He tightens the military-type tourniquet above the belt, though realizes this may not help. Scalise is still talking. He still has a pulse. He is still alive. However, if he keeps losing blood internally, he's going to need a lot of transfusions to his core, heart, lungs, and brain—and it still won't be enough.

When medics arrive, Wenstrup asks for an IV, but they say they don't have one. It's back on the ambulance, and they aren't able to get the ambulance out on the field. Wenstrup gets Scalise to drink a bottle of Gatorade. Scalise is alert enough to say he's very thirsty.

As Scalise is being moved to the ambulance, the paramedics realize how bad he is. If they go in an ambulance, fighting DC traffic, he's not going to make it.

By the time he gets on a Park Police helicopter, he is no longer conscious. But a paramedic has started an IV, and fluid is pouring in.

"I flew Apaches in the war," the pilot says. "I will fly this bird like I stole it."

"There is an inner strength to Steve Scalise," Wenstrup says to me slowly. He tells me what he expects Scalise would have been thinking before he lost consciousness: "Dear God, let me be able to walk my daughter down the aisle someday. Let me live to see that, to do that." Wenstrup says that Scalise talks about this often. "He puts everything in God's hands. I've never seen him angry. I've never seen him bitter. He just looks at what he has to do and prays that he will have the strength to accomplish it."

Congressman Wenstrup feels that his own response to the shooting is influenced by God. "I have my glove. I am going to the outfield. Something comes over me. As I am on my way out there, I stop and turn around and go back to the dugout, get my bat, and go down to the batting cage, which is the safest place I can be and the place where I can observe everything going on. Why do I do that? I mean, I don't even like that batting cage. The machine spitting out balls to hit is wild, and you're always ducking. So why do I go this time? This is a God moment for me. God is directing me. And when the shooting starts, I am able to shelter behind a cinder-block bathroom that is right there and peek out to see what is going on. I am still handling trauma cases as part of my reserve duty, so I am ready to intervene. I automatically know what to do. That's why I am there."

When Scalise gets to the hospital, his blood pressure is down to almost zero from the internal bleeding. Wenstrup says, "I remember a soldier in Iraq who had his blood pressure drop from damage to the iliac arteries, and when we opened him up, there was blood everywhere, and the blood pressure had dropped way down. That soldier didn't make it."

☙

"STEVE IS GOING to need a lot of surgery. But first they have to stop the bleeding and stabilize him," Wenstrup continues. "The system works at every level within a matter of seconds. Replacing volume, rapid transportation, and getting him into the operating room are all lifesaving moves. The speed with which this can take place in a noncombat support hospital is a miracle."

Scalise is taken to MedStar Washington Hospital Center, in the main part of DC. It's the biggest private hospital in

DC, and they treat a lot of gunshot wounds. Their trauma team has seen injuries like this before. The bullet broke into many pieces, shredding his intestines and tearing holes in his arteries. As they're putting blood into him, it's coming back out in other places. MedStar trauma chief Dr. Jack Sava and his team of surgeons take him to the operating room to start tying everything back together.

Scalise receives over fifty units of blood. Dr. Arshad Khan, director of interventional radiology at MedStar, is called in to locate the source of the bleeding and to try to stop it at the same time. He and his team thread a catheter in through the right femoral artery and then steer it over to the left side. They perform an angiogram to see where the arteries are leaking, and Khan thinks it looks like Van Gogh's painting *Starry Night*, with bleeding happening everywhere. Once he's near the left internal iliac artery, he removes the clamp from that side.

Khan can't completely stop the bleeding right away. But at least he sees exactly where it's coming from. There are multiple sites. He needs to fix the bleeding quickly. He could use gel foam to embolize the entire internal iliac artery, but that's pretty drastic and will shut off blood flow to every single vessel. Plus, it takes a month for the gel foam to be reabsorbed. Instead he uses a smaller microcatheter and puts it in through the right groin. He tracks it right to where the bleeding is actually happening on the left. He uses coils, which are like a jumble of wires, to cause blood clots to form inside the tiny vessels and stop the bleeding one vessel at a time. Once the coils or plugs are in, he can then clip the vessels from the outside, and it won't bleed anymore. He does this successfully to two or three branches, and all at once the bleeding stops.

Khan tells me in an interview that he thinks a higher authority must be watching over Scalise. The anesthesiologist expects Scalise to continue to worsen, but as Khan does his final embolization, the anesthesiologist asks, "Did you do something?"

Scalise's blood pressure suddenly stabilizes as the bleeding stops.

The whole procedure takes about forty-five minutes, and then Dr. Jack Sava and his trauma surgery team take back over. They begin to repair the rest of the blood vessels, the intestines, and the damaged tissue. It is a very difficult operation, the first of several.

مـ

SAVA HAS A slight build and a thin jawline, smiling eyes, and a soft, unassuming voice, not the grizzled stereotype for a powerful surgeon, but these stereotypes are luckily receding into the past. "This is a bunch of people who do this over and over again and get supported by the hospital for it," he tells me in a Zoom interview. "Luckily the medical world has supported the advancement of trauma care, the creation of these rapid triage systems, the helicopter that's at the ready, the training system that teaches my team what to do. The end result is that some incredibly sick people can live. Yet despite the best possible care that we can deliver, when Scalise rolls in we realize right away the likelihood of death is ninety percent or more."

Speed is the immediate goal. "We yell about it. We have whole meetings about whether a response could have happened two minutes faster. It's all about getting out of the trauma unit and into the operating room. We don't do trauma in the ER like most places. The fascinating thing about trauma is that you have to undo the entire way that people have been trained to be a doctor since Hippocrates and Galen and before, which is a slow, methodical, stepwise approach. Take a thorough history. Draw some preliminary conclusions. You know we don't do any of that here. We throw all that out the window. Instead, we start with the basic idea of, like, what could kill you within a minute? Is your airway blocked? Let's rule that out. And we need to quickly manage your bleeding because bleeding could kill you within minutes. The team has to hurtle towards stopping the bleeding, and that means ignoring whatever other physical, mental, or emotional noises are occurring in the room. Somebody could have a dagger poking out of their arm; their wife could be screaming in the corner. The patient could be in the most pain of their life. We have to *not* focus on that. Instead, we need to laser-focus on whether you are going to die in the next minutes from bleeding. What do we need to do to stop that? And usually, it means surgery. Sometimes it means interventional radiology. In this case, it means both of those things. This almost never happens in the exact way that it happens with Scalise. There's your miracle."

"Wow," I say. "This sounds a lot like my training days at Bellevue Hospital." Sava smiles and nods.

"If you're talking about a big artery," he says, "then you can just ligate it [tie it off], and you may be done. The problem in this case is a combination of arterial damage to large branches of the big arteries on both sides of the pelvis, and massive destruction to a lot of soft tissue and muscle. So, we can't just take away blood flow from the area, because the tissue would become necrotic and die. Instead, we need to control the bleeding with large clamps and roll him to interventional radiology with the clamps sticking out of his body. This almost never happens, but it is necessary with Scalise. Interventional radiology then gains arterial access, puts their catheter in until they are poking up right against the clamps, removes the clamps, and then they are able to do superselective embolization [closing off] of the tiny vessels that are actually bleeding, rather than upstream blocking of everything. Scalise's case is very risky and it is unique. We almost never work hand in glove with interventional radiology in the middle of an open abdomen. It goes really smoothly with both teams collaborating. Absolutely elegant."

؂

DR. ARSHAD KHAN attended medical school in Pakistan and went on to do extensive training in the US in his field. I speak with him via Zoom. He is in between cases, wearing his scrubs, yet eager to talk. Like Sava, he says Scalise is the most gratifying and challenging case he has ever worked on.

Like Sava, I can tell right away that he is comfortable with himself and with his skills. Khan cannot remember another time when a patient has been brought from the OR to the invasive radiology suite with the clamps sticking out of his abdomen. "The pelvis has a very rich blood flow to it. His injury is not to the main artery. It is to the iliac artery branches, as Dr. Sava told you. These arteries supply the bladder, the rectum, and all the pelvic organs. He has multiple injuries to these branches and surgery cannot reach these tiny vessels. And since he is bleeding all over, you can't see exactly where the bleeding is coming from."

Dr. Khan tells me that with all the damage that was done, the outcome is clearly a miracle. Luckily, Khan has an extensive background in trauma too, having trained with one of the top trauma surgeons in the country in Memphis. Trauma is a subspecialty of Khan's, so he is uniquely suited to handle Scalise's complex case as few others can. Khan is also about the same age as Congressman Scalise, and both men are Cub Scout leaders. They will quickly become friends as Scalise recovers, and Khan prays that Scalise will be alive to return to Cub Scout activities with his son, including the Pinewood Derby car races.

꙰

AFTER THE COMBINED surgery and interventional radiology, Scalise is in a coma for three days before he wakes up and learns what has happened.

Full recovery takes several months. "It is a bumpy course,"

Dr. Sava says, "and I tell Steve's wife, Jennifer, that every day is going to be a bit better than the previous day. His resuscitation and metabolic management are complicated. He has spiking lactate [acid] levels, which tells me that something is horribly wrong. He has many repeat operations with an open abdomen, and it takes a long time to fully close it. His lactate keeps going up, and we keep thinking he is badly infected or the tissue inside is dying from lack of blood flow, but then it turns out he has a hair trigger for it. There are a few infections along the way. His femoral head is shattered, and he has a lot of embedded fragments in his bone. His X-ray shows a Christmas tree of metal fragments all across his pelvis.

"That kind of big bullet is a very powerful weapon that leaves all its kinetic energy in the body. It explodes inside. We don't know if he is ever going to be able to walk again. But he continues to work and make progress to a degree that I don't dare hope for. His courage and his prayer are converted into grit and play a really big role. Steve Scalise is a man of great optimism and of gratitude. We joke about how optimistic he is, and I say he's being ridiculous. I draw him a graph of possible outcomes with likelihoods, and he chooses the one with the tiniest most positive likelihood and says, 'Oh yeah, that's what's happening.' And I think, How am I going to manage his denial? But lo and behold, what he wants is what actually happens. He pushes through the psychic burden; his faith drives him and keeps him from folding up shop the way many people do. He manifests gratitude to God and it directly helps in his recovery."

Sava describes how hard Scalise works to keep his muscles from atrophying, as his nerves, which were damaged by the bullet fragments, slowly recover. Scalise is very weak, and there is a high likelihood that he will never be able to walk again, but he fights through it. Even months after his injury, he is still using a scooter, "and he tires easily. But he continues to work and eventually comes all the way back."

"I am in the hospital for about three and a half months," Scalise says to me. "It is a very long recovery. I have to learn how to walk again. There has been a lot of damage. The bullet went into my left hip. There is damage to my left foot, and they had to put a rod into my left femur because it was shattered. The ball and socket of my hip were severely damaged, so I can't bear any weight for about a month. And there are a lot of other hurdles for me to get through. Other infections have set in as a result of the bullet. There are many dicey moments.

"I am in a wheelchair and then a scooter and then crutches. I do get to go to the Capitol and fly back home to see my family. Finally, I can walk on my own strength."

Great surgical skill combines with timely intervention and unwavering faith to help Scalise recover.

"I put all my focus into getting better and not harping on what happened that day. I lean heavily on my faith. When I was lying on the ball field and couldn't move, and my arms gave out, I decided I was just going to pray and put this in God's hands. I prayed that I would get to see my family again. I felt the presence of God. I'd already been hit, and I couldn't move. There was an all-out gunfight going on, and over a hundred rounds had been fired. For all I knew, the next shot could hit me, and I would be done. But I never felt fear. Once I put my life in God's hands, an unbelievable calm and ease came over me. My mind went to a different place. Whatever was going to happen that day was up to God, and he got me through, and I felt him throughout my recovery."

The shooting and Scalise's struggle to survive have permanently changed his approach to life.

"The day-to-day drama doesn't affect me anymore because I know that that's not really what matters. What's really important is your faith and your family. I don't let anything get me down or knock me off my focus."

"He is humble, not entitled," Dr. Sava says. "Grateful, warm, kind. Both Scalise and his wife really have the ability to connect with people. They are close to the nurses in the trauma ward. They end up close to the rehab people too. They have the ability to forge connections, making the best possible experience out of the most catastrophic health care condition. Afterwards, they put on a giant barbecue for the whole hospital, with New Orleans food flown in. There is literally no one on this medical campus who doesn't want to help them just because of how good they are. Regardless of politics."

꙳

DR. KHAN BELIEVES strongly in medical miracles. "A miracle is something that happens when you've given up hope.

Sometimes when you think nothing is going to save this person, when there's fifty units of transfusion going on, a massive bleeding protocol, a patient unable to be stabilized in the OR and then somehow surviving, that's basically the definition of a miracle."

Khan says he can't remember a previous case that required such extensive embolization (placing of the coils) to stop bleeding in the middle of an operation. Patients in this condition never make it. This case is unheard-of, Khan says. But not only does Scalise survive, he rises out of his wheelchair and returns to Congress.

Congressman Wenstrup (retired January 2025) says, "People ask me, what's the greatest moment that I can share of my time in Congress? And I say, it's when Steve Scalise recovers enough from the shooting to walk back onto the floor of the House of Representatives."

⚘

IN THE SUMMER of 2023, Congressman Scalise notices that his energy level is down dramatically. His wife, Jennifer, convinces him to see the doctor, and they run some tests and diagnose Scalise with multiple myeloma, which used to be almost universally fatal. But now there are therapies that are extremely effective. "Within a day, I am on chemotherapy that quickly turns the cancer around. And within two months my cancer levels have dropped to almost zero. My approach is like everything else I've dealt with—I put it in God's hands. And one of the things God does is present you with options. He'll bring doctors into your life. He brings things into your life that can help you get through it. And I do a stem cell transplant at MD Anderson in Houston. And I develop a much stronger immune system, and then I am in remission. I am still in remission now, and I get checked every month, but it is amazing. In six months, I go from diagnosis to remission.

"It takes a lot of energy and a lot of faith to get better. Prayer plays a big role. I think I am the luckiest man to be alive. I shouldn't have made it through, a few times now, and I attribute it to my faith and a positive mental attitude. It's given me strength to recover, whether it's from a shooting or a cancer diagnosis.

"There are very different types of challenges to face. But with each one of them, I need to have a game plan, and in each case, there are experts and doctors who come into my life to get me through. They are selfless. They are healers. And prayers from friends and strangers help me. It's amazing. And you never know about this invisible network until a stranger says, 'You know, my friend has cancer; would you pray for them?' And you'll pray for a stranger, and you may not know if it affects them. I am fortunately in a place where I have people come up to me, and I'll be in another city, and somebody will say, 'I prayed for you when you were shot' or 'when I heard you had cancer.' And I tell them it's a strong presence, and I feel these prayers, and it's hard to explain, but for people who wonder, Hey, I might be praying for somebody else that I don't know, does it impact them? And I can tell you, it has impacted me in a very positive way."

Scalise is still going for monthly evaluations but says he is completely out of the woods now. His wife and family remain his anchor. "Many times, with the recovery from my gunshot wound and again with my cancer, it is my wife who notices when something is wrong and alerts the doctors."

Former Congressman Wenstrup is in awe of his friend's ability to overcome all odds. "Steve's support structure and faith leads to his courage and strength. It leads directly to his ability to recover."

Scalise's stiff formal posture contrasts with his wide-open smile and relaxed facial expressions, which invite discussion and a warm exchange.

"Sometimes there are true miracles that are the only explanation for something that happens," he says. "I think about this all the time. A shooter arrives in the early morning with the element of surprise and unlimited ammunition, and he desires to kill everybody on that ballfield. And then consider that at the end of this day, everybody's alive except for the shooter; few would think that's possible without a miracle. The heroes are the participants in that miracle, Dr. Wenstrup and Dr. Sava and Dr. Khan, who make sure that people like me and others make it through the day and survive.

"God performs miracles in a lot of different ways. He guides advances in medicine. We see things today that ten years ago would have been unthinkable. Modern-day miracles. God finds brilliant people to carry out his will."

CHAPTER 15

Shane

SHANE DENNEHY IS A TWENTY-TWO-YEAR-OLD college senior at the State University of New York at Binghamton in 2019, thinking about a career as a physician's assistant, when he travels to Punta Cana in the Dominican Republic on a school sponsored trip and dives off the back of a recreational boat. He is very active in water sports and adept at them and doesn't hesitate before diving headfirst off the slide at the back, but this time he hits his head on the bottom. Shane is only dazed at first and makes it back to the boat, where he is holding on to the side when someone on board turns the engine back on. No one is supposed to be starting the boat, but there is a key in the ignition and someone on board turns it without thinking. Shane is sucked up into the turning propeller, badly damaging his leg.

The boat automatically shuts off when the propeller feels resistance. By then the propeller is already buried deep in his leg, and he is bleeding profusely. He passes out from the blood loss and pain.

Shane has "bulked up" in the months before the accident and the additional muscle may provide a wedge between the propeller and his crucial nerves and arteries that are missed by just a few millimeters. If he'd cut his femoral artery, he would have bled out in the water. If he'd cut his sciatic nerve, his leg would no longer work.

Luckily for Shane, two of his friends are medics and they jump in the water and pull him off the propeller and apply a tourniquet to the leg. They pull him out of the water and remove the propeller, which could have been a major mistake because the process of removing it risks severing a major vessel or nerve.

A newly married couple is passing in a speedboat. They've seen everything happen. They have a first-aid kit and a tourniquet, which his friends apply. The couple pulls Shane into the speedboat, and they take him and his four friends to shore. They find a lifeguard stand with a gurney, run the gurney back to the boat, and move Shane onto it. Then they all run with the gurney a mile down the beach until they can find an opening to get to the street. And then they flag down a random taxi van and just scream, "Hospital, hospital, hospital!"

Shane is taken from the initial hospital to a bigger hospital, where some wires are inserted into his leg surgically to try to stabilize the wound. He receives blood transfusions to counter the substantial blood he has lost from the propeller gouging him. One of his friends on the trip contacts Shane's parents (his father is a captain in the New York City Fire Department), who insist they will find a way to get him home. He remains in the Dominican Republic for more than twenty-four hours while his parents frantically arrange for a medical transport plane to bring him back to a top New York City hospital. He is then airlifted to New York–Presbyterian/Weill Cornell Medical Center.

"I have a fractured femur and a shattered hip," Shane says. "And then I have all the muscle loss. The surgeons tell me that they will have to debride large amounts of dead tissue and cut it away. I know it will take many surgeries to try to save this leg."

Shane says the surgeons initially give him "less than five percent chance of keeping the leg. They don't know what they can do, but they will try everything possible."

⚐

DR. JASON SPECTOR is the chief of plastic and reconstructive surgery at Weill Cornell Medicine in New York City. He was a medical student, a surgery resident, and a plastic surgery fellow at NYU Medical Center throughout the 1990s and up until 2006. I knew him then and he had a stellar reputation. Whenever I had a patient with a complex wound infection, there was no one better to call than Dr. Spector. Dr. David Wellman is an orthopedic surgeon practicing at New York–Presbyterian Hospital in Manhattan in 2019. Spector has movie-star good looks, with a long, manly face and a full head of hair that recipients of cosmetic facial plastic surgery would hope for as a result. Wellman also has boyish good looks, thick dark hair, and a confident expression.

Wellman isn't the trauma orthopedist on call at New York–Presbyterian/Weill Cornell Medical Center, in Manhattan, when Shane comes in, but he soon takes the case over and contacts Dr. Spector. They double-team the patient after this.

When I interview them via Zoom, they appear quite comfortable together, finishing each other's sentences, and it is clear to me they could still respond to an emergency call and work together at a moment's notice. They are a Batman-and-Robin team of surgeons, with either capable of functioning as Batman at a given point of a case and the other quickly filling the role of Robin.

Regarding the preliminary surgeries done in the Dominican Republic, Wellman says, "From an orthopedic standpoint, I wish they had done less. They put a bunch of wires into his hip that serve no purpose whatsoever. The first thing we do at Cornell is undo everything they did. Take all of it out . . . and we ultimately put the leg in an ex fix, which is a pin system that jacks the hip back out to length. (This intervention is made early to keep the affected leg from being shorter than the other one.) The next steps involve repeated cleaning of the wound, and I get involved because I am going to be the one who ultimately reconstructs this hip. So, I do a few of the washouts of the wound, and then ultimately I perform the reconstruction once the tissues are ready. Spector does the rest."

Wellman shows me X-rays of the leg taken when Shane arrives at the hospital, and I can see that the long wires that the Dominican surgeons put in were simply an attempt to hold the wound together. Wellman tells me that Shane is lucky the wires didn't puncture an organ or blood vessel.

"This propeller nearly killed him," Wellman says. "Exactly to the millimeter, that's how far the propeller is away from everything. You've got the femoral artery, the femoral nerve, and the sciatic nerve that are all exposed. I've never seen anything like it before or since."

Spector first sees Shane two days after he arrives at New York–Presbyterian/Weill Cornell Medical Center. Spector describes the initial wound as appearing a lot like a battlefield blast injury. Wellman shows me the devastating first photo over Zoom. "Now that's dead beef-jerky-looking muscle there that needs to come off," Spector says. "But because of the force of the injury, things continue to die over the next week or so. And I have to continually go back to the OR to clean it up, to debride. This allows what is still alive to begin to heal and also prevents infection. All of the hamstring muscles are dead. And when I first look at this, I say, there's no way this leg is going to be salvageable. Even though the foot is still being perfused [with blood], and the bottom of the foot has normal sensation and normal motion, which means that the sciatic nerve is still intact and that the main blood supply is still intact, despite how awful this looks. That's why we try, but we know everything has to go exactly right for our attempts to succeed."

Spector moves the dead hamstring muscles out of the way, and he can see that the sciatic nerve is still fine; he can see it exposed and shimmering right before him, an absolute miracle. "This explains why he still has sensation and still has motion below this injury. Once I see this, I think we might conceivably be able to salvage this leg after all. It is just a pipe dream at first, but we certainly are going to try."

Spector brings Shane back to the OR every few days and continues to have the wound debrided, with dead tissue removed and everything cleaned and washed out with a sterile solution. Each step leads to another step without any assurance that it will ever get to a place of real healing. The risk of a high-level amputation and a life spent in a wheelchair continues to loom. At any moment, the whole leg may need to be amputated.

There is a large bony injury to the hip as well, Spector says. "But the problem is he still has this huge chunk of tissue missing. He has a huge orthopedic injury underneath, and this has to get fixed by Dr. Wellman, and then it has to get covered in just the right way so the orthopedic hardware doesn't become infected. . . . I think he is going to need a muscle transplant from another part of his body to cover this. This ends up being the case. This is an extremely tenuous situation."

Reconstructive microsurgery for lower extremity salvage is done all the time. However, this degree of damage presents an enormous challenge to both surgeons. "In this scenario, with all this damage, even though the main arterial supply is clearly intact, most of the adjacent blood supply that we need to attach to the tissue is gone. We don't know what to do at first," Spector says.

After several days, Dr. Wellman finally performs surgery, an open reduction and internal fixation to the hip that Dr. Spector calls "beautiful." This procedure involves realigning the broken bones and holding them together with metal implants. Keeping the hardware that Wellman installs from becoming infected is another great challenge. Spector says the hip area must be colonized with bacteria because it has been an open wound for a few weeks, despite having been cleaned out every two days. Intravenous antibiotics are given as a preventative, in the hope that they penetrate deeply enough into the wound to work. Meanwhile, the surgery interventions continue around the clock. Spector says, "We take the remaining muscles that are in the area and move them to the degree that we can, based upon the amount that their vascular supply will allow. We are very fortunate given his youth and his ability to heal, the fact that we are very diligent in cleaning, moving the muscles around to cover up the hardware aided by the body's natural healing, the wound contracts down over time."

Listening to the story, I find myself grimacing with each setback, cheering with each tenuous step forward. Readers of this book may not know how laborious and painstaking surgery and the healing of severe wounds can be. I barely know it myself. I have seen devastating wounds throughout my career, especially while working in the Bellevue Hospital emergency room. But once I've helped to stabilize a patient, they are whisked off to the operating room, and the step-by-step repairs that come later occur outside my field of view or influence. Very few wound repairs are more extensive or laborious or unlikely to succeed than Shane's.

Over the two weeks since Shane first came to Weill Cornell on March 23, Wellman has put the bone back into place, and Spector's meticulous work finally begins to pay off. The wound looks better and Spector decides it is time to try to close it and "put a skin covering on it." Shane remains in significant pain, but he is taking opioids, which help. He is bearing some weight on the leg and physical therapy starts to help too. Wellman marvels that he has gotten this far. He says he has never seen anything like it.

There are still many setbacks. Spector chooses not to do a skin graft right away because he is afraid it won't take hold. Instead he creates an artificial "dermal template." This is a thick collagen layer that is wrapped around the wound, creating a foundation for the body to receive a real skin graft later. Things are finally looking good, and Spector says they think they "may just get away with doing this, but then the inevitable happens, and Shane starts to leak some pus from the wound."

Plus, in doing the washouts, they hit live muscle this time, and it bleeds, and the surgeons worry now there is only a small chance they can possibly do all the surgeries needed to repair the leg. They need more viable tissue to attach their repairs to.

Disaster looms. With the possibility of a deeper, dangerous infection that will lead directly to immediate amputation, the two great doctors confer and manage to find another creative solution. They bring in muscle tissue from the other leg (a flap) with its substantial blood supply attached to help heal the infected tissue. At the same time, Wellman introduces beads that are loaded with antibiotics right into the wound. The hardware that Wellman has put into the hip is being colonized by bacteria, but the infused antibiotics and the new muscle flap and blood supply help to fight back and protect the reconstructed joint before it becomes badly infected. "We connect the blood vessels from the muscle flap to his femoral artery," Spector says, "so that the infected area receives a fresh blood supply and the immune cells to fight the infection."

It is now six weeks after the initial injury. The two doctors hold their breath.

It works. The infection in the wound, in the surrounding tissue, and in the reconstructed joint slowly abates. More skin grafts are added, and two months after the original injury, it all starts to come together. Wellman proudly shows me a photo taken at this time, and I am amazed at how improved the leg is, with the red streaks (from skin grafts) looking like patches on a tire.

High-level amputation is barely avoided over and over. More miracles are still to come if Shane is ever going to be able to walk again, let alone perform water sports.

"Just looking at his bony injury, I think he is never going to be able to walk again," Spector says. "I would bet on it."

"This is an incredibly tough injury for us," Wellman says. "Any time you get a femoral neck fracture at the top of the thigh . . . especially high-energy, open, infected, contaminated femoral neck. I mean, you're looking at a very high failure rate. Extremely likely, our attempts to reconstruct the bone will not work."

Wellman continues: "You can see how much bone he's missing. Our goal is to build a construct that gives the leg stability and can last long enough for the big fracture to heal. We know we are very likely to fail, but we keep our heads down and never look beyond the next step in the process. That's the secret to never giving up. In this case, you clean, you clean, you clean. Getting debris, getting dead tissue out of there. And the timing is so important. You can't just put a bunch of metal—the implant—in there. It will quickly get infected. I need to wait until Dr. Spector is ready to cover up the implants I put in and rotate muscle around them so the metal is not exposed. It is a constant, coordinated effort. Two teams working together and communicating in a hospital where it's quite difficult to align surgical services. But we work together like a hand and a glove."

Wellman shows me a photo of all the missing bones in Shane's leg. "You can see all the white areas where bone ought to be," he says. "And so, we sequentially just start to put the pieces back together, reconstructing something that looks like a hip. We actually borrow metal plates and hardware (from a separate section in the hospital), which are designed to treat fractures around total hip replacements, and we use a combination of their implants and plates and screws. Thankfully, with fractures, if you can get one of the dominant columns of bone to heal, typically the rest of it will fill in and heal around it. We get very, very lucky."

The future of Shane's leg and his quality of life still hang in the balance, as the two teams begin to score one success after another. It is like skiing just ahead of an avalanche. Momentum builds but the outcome is never guaranteed.

After multiple debridements and cutting out dead tissue,

Spector finally creates a clean wound bed with enough muscle there to cover up the implants Wellman has placed. He again places antibiotic beads to fight any infection that may show up. Miraculously there are no holes, no dead space. They don't need to take the metal implants out. The leg is slowly coming back together.

"It is a true miracle," Dr. Wellman says. "This is the most astounding case I've ever worked on. We never imagine at the beginning that the guy will ever be running again, playing basketball."

If Wellman had to amputate, Shane would have to spend much of his life in a wheelchair. Instead, "you would not know what happened if you meet him," Wellman says.

مله

THE ACCIDENT OCCURRED in March 2019, and I join Shane via Zoom in June 2024 and ask him how he is doing now. "I walk down the street, and there is no limp." He shows me his healed leg proudly. "I remember when I first got to the hospital, they told me I would likely never be able to walk or run again. Sports for you are done, they said. At best, you're going to walk with a bad limp, with leg length discrepancy. We will have to get a boost in your shoes because it's going to be off. But I got none of that. Everything's good. I play sports, I snowboard, I wakeboard." Shane is also back on boats, and he is waterskiing. He has fully returned to the very activities that caused the need for his medical miracle in the first place. His personal courage is inspiring.

Shane says that staying positive throughout and his faith in God have helped him through. "I believe in a higher power. This definitely pushed the envelope and something helped me to get here. I'm grateful to be here. I tell everyone every day's an extra day for me. I'm living on borrowed time at this point."

He shows me the one big wide scar that remains. Initially the skin grafts were bright red, but they have gradually faded, and now he says, "the skin itself looks fantastic." He shows me that he is still missing a lot of muscle at the back and outside of his upper leg and that "half my left butt is gone."

Shane tells me that the experience influenced him to become a surgical physician's assistant. "I've always been comfortable in the OR. . . . Now, I see patients in the hospital, and they tell me about all the pain they have. And I can relate. And when they're stuck, and stop to improve, or when they have revision surgeries, I understand and try to help them move forward." Through the whole experience of his recovery, Shane was working with the team and imagining himself as a physician's assistant helping others in his predicament.

"I thought he was going to lose his leg," Dr. Spector says. "I was ninety-eight to ninety-nine percent sure he was going to lose it. I was extremely surprised that it worked out. Not only that we saved his leg, but he's as active as he is. And then, on top of everything, he bonded with my physician's assistant, who was very active in taking care of him in the hospital and then communicated with him as an outpatient. And this inspired and motivated Shane. He saw the crucial role that the PA played in taking care of him and other patients, and the next thing I knew, he was at St. John's PA school. And then he reached out to me and asked if he could rotate with us. And I said, yeah, sounds cool. You know, I've never had a patient do this before. And then he gets a job at our place, Hospital for Special Surgery, and when I go over there to operate, I run into Shane. Imagining his own future in the medical field gave him something to look forward to and helped him to recover."

Spector says he felt a little like he was working on the leg of Frankenstein's monster as he kept doing surgery after surgery over the months to make the leg look better, inserting tissue expanders and silicone water balloons. Spector says the medical-grade saline-filled expanders not only stretched the skin but also induced new skin to form.

Finally, Spector removed the expanders. Once all the new skin had been made, he "got rid of the ugly, thin skin graft and advanced the expanded new skin to cover the muscle." It was looking closer and closer to a normal leg, and most importantly, it was starting to function as one.

Years later, Shane continues to send Dr. Spector photos of his waterskiing, and Spector continues to marvel, like a sculptor who can't believe what he's made.

At each juncture, there was another chance of limb-threatening infection or a nonhealing muscle, skin graft, or bone. In its place, there was a gradual progression to recovery as the number of scars diminished and the leg once again became capable of high-tension water sports. Rarely are medical miracles possible without the most gifted of healers involved. Healers who possess the hands of God. These were two of the very best.

"I miss you, Dr. Wellman," Dr. Spector says.

"Oh, I miss you," Dr. Wellman says with tears in his eyes. "I so wish we were still doing this stuff together."

☙

I WISH I could end this chapter by saying that there are new controls or restrictions placed over recreational boating in the Caribbean and elsewhere as a result of Shane's story, but the rampant use of slides at the back of these boats with associated devastating injuries continues. And sometimes the miracles are to be found not just in the actual treatments or surgeries, but also in getting the patient into the right hands.

On New Year's Eve, 2022, I receive a text from a top Fox executive, Sue Kinzie, that her dear friend Mark's son, Aidan Lotruglio, age twenty-one, has sustained a severe accident while on vacation, diving headfirst down a slide at the back of a recreational boat, also in Punta Cana, Dominican Republic. Like Shane, Aidan is a young man who loves water sports. Aidan badly miscalculates, and, also like Shane, he hits his head hard on the shallow bottom. But Aidan hits his head much harder. Miraculously, he is still able to walk and still has all sensation in his feet and hands, but several hours later a CT scan at a local hospital shows a severely fractured spinal column. It is a miracle that he isn't yet paralyzed. Mark Lotruglio texts me the CT scan images. When I see them, I decide to try to bring him to Miami, a particularly difficult task to accomplish on New Year's Eve.

Aidan lacks a proper neck brace in the local DR hospital

and is allowed to walk unaided to the bathroom. Luckily, his pain functions as a warning sign to keep him from moving too much, which would irreversibly damage his spinal cord. A single wrong move from an unfettered broken neck would be enough to finish him.

He is sequestered unmonitored in a room. With each hour that passes, his wiggling toes and fingers seem more of a miracle. Finally, he finds a cell phone to contact his worried parents and they contact me and together we begin the long process of transferring him via medevac back to the United States early in the morning on January 1.

On New Year's Day in Miami, Dr. Allan Levi, renowned chief of neurosurgery at the University of Miami's Miller School of Medicine, is there at Jackson Memorial Hospital in Miami ready to receive young Aidan. He operates for several hours, putting in titanium hardware to fortify both the front and back of Aidan's cervical spine.

When I speak to Levi, he says that Aidan is among the "small percent of patients" with this kind of injury who don't have neurological deficits from spinal cord damage. But Levi is also struck by all that had to go exactly right to get him to Miami. 'He was really lucky to be able to hold his neck still, without external immobilization. Now, if he got jostled or jolted or pushed or fell, you know, that could have been the end of it. That's probably the biggest miracle. That there wasn't any further damage after his original trauma despite his walking to the bathroom, no proper neck brace, etc., etc."

Levi says that the pain and clenching of his neck muscles while still in the Dominican Republic save Aidan from paralysis because "it basically creates an internal brace for his neck that prevents him from dislocating it further."

Several months of expert rehabilitation at Jackson Memorial Hospital Rehabilitation follow the surgery, and in May 2023 Aidan walks to the podium at Washington and Lee University in Virginia to receive his college degree in business administration.

Like Shane, Aidan is an athlete who played many sports growing up, including soccer in high school. Following the accident and his recovery, he returns to playing golf and wakeboarding. In April 2024 he completes a half-marathon in around one hour and forty-five minutes. Like Shane, he fully recovers.

CHAPTER 16

Back from the Dead

THERE IS NO DOUBT THAT modern technology has greatly improved our ability to diagnose death, whether it is based on the brain no longer functioning or the heart ceasing to beat, as is currently the method we physicians use here in the US to declare the cessation of life. But a physician must actually be present to declare someone dead; in fact, I have declined to sign many death certificates when I haven't been in attendance. Perhaps one day soon, an AI-driven robot will take a physician's place not only in terms of signing death certificates but also in conducting autopsies to determine the cause. In the meantime, the role falls on physicians, and one of the best in the business for decades has been forensic pathologist Dr. Michael Baden. Baden has long been the go-to expert opinion on high-profile deaths, including the JFK assassination. But Baden also points out to me in an interview that dead isn't always really dead.

Dr. Baden says that in his long experience as a medical examiner and top forensic pathologist, a person coming

THE MIRACLES AMONG US

back from being declared dead only occurs once every ten to twenty years. But what is truly disturbing is that according to Baden, "even with the invention [in 1902] and the regular utilization of EKG machines in the 1960s, they are still not routinely used at first to determine if a patient's heart has stopped beating before sending them to the morgue." This is truly sloppy medical care. Baden tells me about one case that may seem to involve divine intervention (with God showing us his sense of humor), even if Baden himself resists the use of the term *miracle*.

"When I start in Manhattan at the medical examiner's office in the 1960s, there is a heavyset white male in his sixties brought in from a nearby downtown hospital for heart disease who is found dead in the morning when nurses do their rounds. The man's family has already been complaining bitterly and repeatedly to the hospital authorities about the poor care he is receiving, so you can imagine how they react when he suddenly dies.

"The man is Pickwickian, meaning that he has a lot of fat tissue around his upper chest and neck and that he breathes shallowly [obesity-hypoventilation syndrome], leading to a buildup of carbon dioxide. The man has heart disease and sustains a heart attack, and his family can't believe that his complaints of chest pain in the hospital are being ignored.

"The nurses find him one morning not breathing, and declare him dead. They load him in the morgue wagon and ship him over. On the way, the driver hears some strange moaning sounds and isn't sure where they are coming from. He doesn't tell anyone because he thinks he will be accused of imagining things. At the morgue, the man is put in the cooler for four hours prior to the autopsy. When he is taken out of there, the body bag is opened, and they put him on the metal table, the slab. His hands move.

"I yell to the attendants, and they quickly rush him back to the hospital, where the family is now even more irate."

This time they keep him on a heart monitor all the time, and they watch him more closely and give him oxygen. They think they are being ultra careful after what happened the first time. He doesn't wake up, but he makes more sounds that he hasn't made before. The family still hopes he may stir and wake up. He is in the ICU for two days, but then nurses and doctors at the hospital think he has stopped breathing. They look for a pulse and find none, and so he "dies" again, and again an EKG is not taken and again he is brought back to the morgue. Again he is making agonal sounds on the way, and again he is put in cold storage for four hours in a body bag. Again he is put on the metal autopsy table. Again he moves.

"No way I am cutting into him," Dr. Baden says. "I have seen people wrongly pronounced dead, but never twice with the same patient. I don't think anyone has. Keep in mind that in those days, the nurses make the determination of death by checking a pulse and for lack of breathing, but it is much harder to determine in someone who is Pickwickian. You can barely tell he is breathing to begin with.

"But the second time he comes in, I know he is alive because I hear the sounds again coming from the mouth even though you can't tell he's breathing, and I groan, 'Oh no.'

We all hear the sounds; one of the morgue men recognizes the body—and pays attention to movement in the fingers.

"So I send him back to the hospital again a second time. You can imagine how the family feels. They are apoplectic."

I ask Baden about the air in the body bag and he says there is a little, very little. But the body bags are often reused several times, so there are holes in them. If you're breathing, there should be no problem getting sufficient air through the holes.

"I truly can't believe they don't use EKGs to prevent this from happening," I say. He replies, "In the sixties, we use them on living patients—we don't use them on dead people. If we don't see evidence of breathing, we don't get the EKGs. I know that's wrong, but that's protocol. Nowadays you go to a scene, a patient is only pronounced dead with an EKG. In those days, if someone is found lifeless in the morning, six a.m. is when they usually make rounds. That's when people are declared dead. Keep in mind that rigor mortis, or stiffening of the body, comes on around three to four hours after death and starts in the small muscles in the mouth after one to two hours—if you try to open the mouth, you can find it. That can also happen from the cold, from the fridge. You have to gently open the mouth. I do that with him, with all of them. People don't routinely look for it back then, but I look for it. He doesn't have it. No rigor mortis."

So Baden sends the man back to the hospital again, and everyone expects him to wake up this time.

"Does he?" I ask.

"No," Baden says. "He stays in a coma for a few days, making sounds and moving, but he never fully wakes up, and finally he dies. But the last time, they finally use an EKG to make sure he doesn't have a heart rhythm after the second time when he probably did, and they missed it. So, the third time he comes to us, he is really dead. Brains die first—twenty percent of the body's oxygen goes to the brain. But sometimes people come out of comas. An EKG, if done properly combined with no pulse, declares death on this basis in the US. Sometimes a dead person looks like a live person. In this man's case, a live person looked like a dead one—twice. I honestly think this case helps the hospital decide to use an EKG machine to determine death. But it should have been done long before this.

"I remember when Dr. Milton Helpern was chief medical examiner before I was, and just when he was making the incision going into the chest, someone flinched. A body was found dead in the street; they thought he was an alcoholic. They put him up on the table. He had sclerosis of the liver. Put the scalpel to the chest—the person jumped."

Baden tells me that often it isn't how a person dies that is the mystery but how they manage to live with so much illness. Cancer patients are doing normal activities the day before they die despite massive damage to their organs, and even some Alzheimer's patients act perfectly normal despite extreme damage to their brains. "One person has coronaries with zero blood flow to their heart whatsoever, yet manages to live that way," Baden says.

"Sometimes the wrong person is declared dead. Then the person who is wrongly declared dead but is really still alive makes away with the insurance money."

Baden is the maven of bizarre death miracles. "I remember one sunny day in Queens five people die with different athletic activities. And there are five different pairs of shoes in the autopsy room. It is often athletic activity rather than sedentary activity that kills people," Baden says. "I have photos of five different pairs of shoes—running, tennis, golf, a baseball player—and it convinces me that exercise is the Devil's own making. If you sit at home you are safe."

"No internist or cardiologist agrees with you on that," I say, and Baden chuckles. Dr. Baden says he believes in a spiritual reality that is beyond our ability to comprehend, though he considers himself a man of science primarily. But he speaks with a compassionate, soothing voice that he says helps families who have just lost a loved one, including that irate family at the downtown hospital early in Baden's career who lose their loved one three times. This family comments to Baden that it is really sad that the only doctor they trust is the pathologist.

Indeed, it is only Baden, the medical examiner, who is able to soothe many an irate grieving family. Over the course of his long career, Baden's caring voice has helped many on their path to the next world, as well as those who must remain behind in this one.

علم

ONE STEP BEYOND being declared dead when you are still alive is being buried in that condition. According to Dr. Michael Baden, two centuries ago fear of being buried alive was widespread, and being brought back from the dead wasn't always a miracle if you didn't actually die in the first place.

Because so many people were dying or being declared dead rapidly during the cholera epidemics throughout the nineteenth century in Europe, Baden reports that anxiety over premature burial led to the invention of safety devices that could be incorporated into coffins.

Over thirty designs were patented in Germany in the late nineteenth century alone.

The first recorded safety coffin was constructed on the orders of Duke Ferdinand of Brunswick before his death in 1792. He had a window installed to allow light in and an air tube to provide a supply of fresh air, and instead of having the lid nailed down, he had a lock fitted. It could be unlocked from the inside if a mistake was made.

☙

IN 1822, DR. Adolf Gutsmuth of Seehausen, Germany, demonstrated his safety coffin, burying himself underground for several hours and having a full meal through the coffin's feeding tube. His meal included soup, bratwurst, marzipan, sauerkraut, spaetzle, beer, and an elaborate dessert known as prinzregententorte. When he emerged, he was so full he could barely breathe.

Most models of safety coffins had significant design flaws, including that ropes tied to the arms and legs could be triggered by natural movements of the body in death as it putrefied and bloated. So dead people could theoretically set off an alert as well as live people wrongly buried. It is unknown how many of these special coffins were actually used. "Portable death chambers" were tested in the 1820s in Germany. A small chamber, with a bell and a window for viewing the body, was constructed over an empty grave. Watchmen would check for signs of life. If the bell was rung, the "body" could be immediately removed, but if the watchman observed signs of the corpse decomposing, a door in the floor of the chamber could be opened and the body would drop down into the actual grave.

The security coffin designed by Dr. Johann Gottfried Taberger in 1829 was well thought out. It alerted a cemetery night watchman by a bell, which was activated by a rope connected to strings attached to the hands, feet, and head of the body. The bell housing prevented the alarm from going off due to the wind or birds perching on it. There was a tube to keep rainwater out and a mesh to keep away insects. If the bell went off, a second tube was supposed to be immediately inserted at the bottom of the coffin and air pumped in through a bellows to keep the person alive.

Some safety coffins were even more elaborate. The patent for the "Vester Burial Case" in 1868 stated, "The nature of this invention consists of placing on the lid of the coffin, and directly over the face of the body laid therein, a square tube, which extends from the coffin up through and over the surface of the grave, said tube containing a ladder and a cord, one end of said cord being placed in the hand of the person laid in the coffin, and the other being attached to a bell on the top of the square tube, so that, should a person be

interred ere life is extinct, he can, on recovery to consciousness, ascend from the grave and the coffin by the ladder; or,
if not able to ascend by said ladder, ring the bell, thereby giving an alarm, and thus save himself from premature burial
and death; and, if on inspection, life is extinct, the tube is
withdrawn, the sliding door closed, and the tube used for a
similar purpose [on another body]."

و

FEAR OF BEING declared dead and buried before your time
has long preoccupied some of the greatest pre-twentieth-
century artists and statesmen: "All I desire for my own
burial is not to be buried alive," Lord Chesterfield wrote to
his daughter-in-law on March 16, 1769. "Have me decently
buried, but do not let my body be put into a vault in less
than two days after I am dead," ordered George Washington. "The earth is suffocating. . . . Swear to make them cut
me open, so that I won't be buried alive," Frédéric Chopin,
the great composer, uttered as he died. The fear of premature
burial reached its peak in 1896 when businessman William
Tebb created the London Association for the Prevention of
Premature Burial, a group that advocated for burial reforms
to ensure the dead were truly dead. Due to the cholera out-
breaks, newspapers were filled with accounts of premature
burials. One example from the July 22, 1880, edition of *The
Undertaker's Journal* was truly shocking. A woman was buried alive and gave birth inside her coffin. This is not to say
that all people who were mistakenly buried alive automatically

represented medical miracles or that they literally returned from the dead and a lifeless body was reanimated. At the same time, misdiagnosing death by a nonmedical person was quite common in the eighteenth and nineteenth centuries. It frequently involved putting a mirror in front of the patient's nose to see if outgoing breath misted the mirror. Of course, this method was often not sensitive enough. In the twentieth century it became routine for a country's parliament to put regulations in place requiring medical professionals to confirm death before the body was handled by an undertaker. Even then, people were frequently buried alive. Dr. Baden tells me that sometimes you only knew someone was buried alive because an undertaker found scratch marks on the inside of the coffin. By the time he became a medical examiner, the number of people being declared dead prematurely had plummeted, but the case of the Pickwickian man declared dead three times awakened Baden to the fact that the possibility still existed.

المعر

BELIEVE IT OR not, safety coffins are still available today. As recently as 1995, an Italian man, Fabrizio Caselli, invented a model that includes an emergency alarm, a two-way microphone/speaker, a torch, an oxygen tank, a heartbeat sensor, and a heart stimulator.

But safety coffins provide a set of guardrails against calling "game over" prematurely that are really no longer needed and perhaps never really were. After all, life and death is and always has been in God's hands. Throughout this book, God's presence is felt by many of those who have managed to survive against all odds, whether aided by medical science or prayer or both, whether they conform to strict Catholic Church criteria for miracles (extremely unusual), or are in fact one of Cardinal Dolan's so-called soft miracles, or are events guided by a great prophet like the Rebbe. It also doesn't matter whether the miracle is due to direct divine intervention, or God working through the hands of a great physician like medical missionary Tom Catena or trauma surgeon Jack Sava, or simply God playing tricks on us versus the impact of poor medical care, as in the case of Baden's dead man walking. We must remember all the time that "thy life is a miracle," as Edgar says emphatically to his father Gloucester after feigning his death in Shakespeare's great play *King Lear*.

A Prayer for My Patients

THROUGHOUT MY CAREER AS A physician, I have taken care of very sick patients. I have learned that empathy matters as much as any other tool I have to offer. I have learned to combine the spiritual with the physical, often being the last among my peers to give up hope. Being a successful physician means combining the latest technology with careful listening to the patient in the search for a cure.

I remember one patient early in my training who helped me find my path. His name was Charles, and he was overcome by a high fever as his lungs stiffened with pneumonia. His parents and sister were camped by his bedside. They prayed day and night there, even as he slipped into a coma. Charles was only twenty-eight years old and his family resisted the repeated attempts of the hospital to withdraw care. One day when I arrived in his room, I saw that his fever had broken and he opened his eyes, fully aware, as he stared straight at me. Soon he was sitting in a chair and expressing gratitude to me for not giving up on him. "It wasn't my time," he said. "God didn't want me to go yet. He still has a purpose for me in this world."

I worked for years at NYU's Rusk Institute for Rehabilitation Medicine, witnessing many who rose out of wheelchairs who weren't supposed to, or recovered from serious operations or strokes.

No story of recovery was more unlikely than that of my patient Howard, who was told he would never walk again but rose out of a wheelchair to confront a lawyer who he said owed him millions of dollars. Howard shot the man and was sentenced to prison, though he was later found to be too ill to ever serve a day. After Howard, I learned to never doubt what a patient says they can accomplish.

During the tragic devastation of the COVID pandemic, I witnessed many survival stories that could only be explained by God's intervention, including patients who made it off ventilators when few thought they could, while other patients overcame large blood clots and made it home.

God's presence is real whether the patient or doctor recognizes it or not. Dick has been my patient for over thirty years. He says he isn't religious, yet he has experienced one miraculous cure after another in the decades I have cared for him. He has beaten four deadly cancers, heart failure, and more than one life-threatening gastrointestinal bleed. I have supplied the medical quarterbacking and God has done the rest.

To be sure, he has benefited from the latest technology in

his cures, as much as all the subjects of this book have. In his latest foray with cancer, pinpoint-radiation 190 "seed" implantation has completely obliterated the multipronged cancer in his liver. Dick says that "someone must be watching over me."

"Why are you still alive?" I ask him.

"So I can take your phone calls."

Dick still smokes half a pack of cigarettes a day, and says he has no intention of stopping. At the age of eighty-five, he receives intravenous gamma globulin treatments for a peripheral nerve problem, and as a result he is still walking. "My midlife crisis began with prostate cancer, which led to bladder cancer, which led to lung cancer, which led to liver cancer, and today I am cancer-free," he says. "Along the way I overcame heart bypass surgery and a hard-to-find bleed in my intestines that caused my blood counts to go way down. This problem recurs on a regular basis, and each time, I beat it." Regarding smoking, Dick says, "You need to keep doing the few things you really enjoy. All my doctors have asked me to quit but I never have."

My decades of being a physician have taught me that we each have one life and we have to treasure it. God decides how long we have; doctors should not try to usurp that role. God may see a purpose for our remaining in the world that we aren't even aware of. God is looking over Dick and keeping him with us, and my phone calls are only a tiny part of the reason.

There is a central prayer for healing in Judaism, known as Mi Shebeirach. It is a prayer for the sick, that God should heal them. "May the source of strength, who blessed the ones before us, help us find the courage to make our lives a blessing, and let us say, Amen.

"Bless those in need of health, the renewal of body, the renewal of spirit, and let us say, Amen."

We pray for recovery of particular patients, inserting their name into the prayer, but of course in the end God decides.

There is also the great healing prayer of St. Padre Pio, which says in part, "Cast out anything that should not be in me. Root out any unhealthy and abnormal cells. Open any blocked arteries or veins and rebuild and replenish any damaged areas. Remove all inflammation and cleanse any infection by the power of Jesus's precious blood.

"Let the fire of your healing love pass through my entire body to heal and make new any diseased areas so that my body will function the way you created it to function. Touch also my mind and my emotion, even the deepest recesses of my heart."

I remember my very first patient, Anna, whom I saw in the Bellevue Hospital medical clinic for her diabetes. I then followed her for many years in my office practice and she became part of my extended family. I did whatever I could for as long as I could to keep her alive and healthy well into her nineties, and her family saw me as her good luck charm, but I always knew that it was God who was keeping her going.

Patients reveal their secrets to me, whether it is a marriage gone awry or a secret sore or pain or sudden stumble that they worry will be their end. I do my best to comfort them and aid them, and pray for their healing.

Medical technology is my tool as a physician, complemented by prayer and a patient's courage and hope. Miracles come when the physician's hands of God are combined with prayer and these prayers are answered.

I pray for each and every one of you, my patients, my readers, those who watch me on TV or listen to me on the radio. I wish you all good health and a long life. May God save you.

ACKNOWLEDGMENTS

TWO DECADES AGO, in a former editing job, Eric Nelson, now an executive editor at HarperCollins and vice president and publisher of Broadside Books, noticed that I had amassed a prodigious outpouring of op-eds and TV appearances about health scares after 9/11. He conceived of a way for me to weave my insights together into a book on the disproportionate fear response to our new sense of vulnerability and how that fear took over our lives. Now, two decades later, I have the privilege to work with Eric again along with his highly talented associate editor, James Neidhardt. Eric is a brilliant editor, with a highly advanced sense of narrative flow. He brings patchwork manuscripts together to a holistic whole. He is as talented as any nonfiction editor in the business.

Speaking of talent, few can match the creative genius of Lisa Sharkey, senior vice president and creative director at HarperCollins. Her passion and interest in this book are palpable and contagious. She is a great visionary in the book publishing world, and like Eric, she sees books as a whole. She came up with the title *The Miracles Among Us*, the section heads, and the personal prayer section, and she provided much excitement and insight to me on a chapter-by-chapter level. I am very grateful. Many thanks also to Lisa's meticulous and affable assistant editor, Lexie von Zedlitz.

They all made me feel like part of the Harper family. And on the topic of families, I have been part of the Fox family for seventeen years. Rupert and Lachlan Murdoch have long been big supporters of my on-air work. CEO Suzanne Scott has helped me to navigate. She is a big believer in medical miracles and I am extremely lucky to have her in my corner. I am very grateful for her personal interest. Lauren Petterson, president of talent development, is another creative visionary who has long backed my attempts to break new ground both on TV and in print. Vice President of Talent Development Jennings Grant is great at building bridges, at bringing people and concepts together, as is essential when on-air talent is joining with a great publishing house. In my case Jennings has built personal bridges for me with the prodigious team at Harper. My research assistant, Melanie Dadourian, has been very committed to this project, coordinating interviews, digging deep for information, and providing a useful sounding board.

Speaking of families, I want to thank my wife, Ludmilla, and our children, Josh, Rebecca, and Sam, for always standing by me proudly and respecting my investigative attempts into the joint worlds of science and faith. Josh is already a great journalist in his own right, while Sam is a budding filmmaker overflowing with talent. Rebecca is just starting out in medical school, and she too believes in the patient's personal narrative as well as spiritual transcendence. There is always so much more to patient care than vital signs and lab results. She is gathering the tools she needs to transcend boundaries and fight for treatments and cures while believing strongly in the essential role of faith.

My wife has always been guided by courage and steadfastness and an intuitive insight not just in her field of neurophysiology and medicine, where she has saved many lives, but also in the ways she has built a strong family and transmitted these values to our children.

I also want to thank the large number of clergy who have contributed significantly to this book, from Cardinal Dolan, who has taken a personal interest and provided a central message on miracles, to the doctor at Lourdes, to Pastor Sam Rodriguez, to disciples of the Rebbe. My appreciation extends to the entire Osteen clan and their huge Lakewood megachurch in Houston. Several doctors have contributed their miracle stories, and their interviews about their patients are at the heart of this book.

Most of all I want to thank my patients for believing in me and in their own capacity for a miracle recovery. By feeling and responding to God's presence, miracles flow over them and eventually some have made their way onto the pages of this book.

The greatest inspiration for this book is my parents: my father, who is 101, and my mother, who is 100. When asked how he could possibly make it this long, beset by many medical problems, including end-stage kidney disease requiring dialysis, my father says that it is his love for my mother that has kept him alive. They have been married for seventy-three years. It is a real love story, and God has been paying attention.

NOTES

Chapter 2: Damar

20 which Damar himself acknowledges: Michael Merschel, "What Is Commotio Cordis, which NFL Player Damar Hamlin Says Stopped His Heart?" *American Heart Association News*, April 18, 2023, https://www.heart.org/en/news/2023/04/18/what-is-commotio-cordis-which-nfl-player-damar-hamlin-says-stopped-his-heart.

20 97 percent fatal: Luis E. Palacio and Mark S. Link, "Commotio Cordis," *Sports Health* 1, no. 2 (2009): 174–79, doi:10.1177/1941738108330972.

20 more than 60 percent: Barry J. Maron and N. A. Mark Estes, "Commotio Cordis Returns . . . When We Least Expected It: Cardiac Arrest in a Professional Football Player," *American Journal of Cardiology* 202 (2023): 229–32, https://www.ajconline.org/article/S0002-9149(23)00396-X/fulltext.

21 underlying structural heart disease: "Commotio Cordis," *ScienceDirect*, accessed January 10, 2025, https://www.sciencedirect.com/topics/nursing-and-health-professions/commotio-cordis#definition.

21 extremely unlikely: Maron and Estes, "Commotio Cordis Returns."

25 10 percent: Patrick Broadwater and Ellen Goldbaum, "Bills Team Doc Turns Spotlight of Damar Hamlin Injury onto Increasing Bystander CPR/AED Training," *University at Buffalo News*, December 30, 2023, https://www.buffalo.edu/news/releases/2023/12/Bills-team-doc-CPR-AED-training.html.

Chapter 3: Breakthrough

36 less than thirty minutes: SungJoon Park et al., "Optimal Cardiopulmonary Resuscitation Duration for Favorable Neurological Outcomes After Out-of-Hospital Cardiac Arrest," *Scandinavian Journal of Trauma, Resuscitation and Emergency Medicine* 30, no. 5 (2022), https://doi.org/10.1186/s13049-022-00993-8.

37 "oxygen stores to the brain": Alecs H. Chochinov et al., "Recovery

of a 62-Year-Old Man from Prolonged Cold Water Submersion," *Annals of Emergency Medicine* 31, no. 1 (1998): 127–31, https://doi.org/10.1016 /S0196-0644(98)70296-3.

Chapter 4: The Albert Schweitzer of Sudan

45 interview from Kenya: Christine Rousselle, "American Doctor, Fueled by Faith, Brings Health and Healing to Rural Sudan: 'God Is in Charge,'" Fox News, June 14, 2024, https://www.foxnews.com /lifestyle/american-doctor-fueled-faith-brings-health-care-rural-sudan -god-in-charge.

52 NCAA Theodore Roosevelt Award: Nicole Ezeh, "2024 Theodore Roosevelt Award: Dr. Tom Catena," NCAA, December 13, 2023, https://www.ncaa.org/news/2023/12/13/media-center-2024-theodore -roosevelt-award-dr-tom-catena.aspx.

Chapter 5: The Pharmacist and the Baby

57 save the baby: "A Baby, a Heart, and a Dream," rickhodes.org, accessed February 10, 2025, https://rickhodes.org/a-baby-a-heart-and-a-dream.

60 no word for Down syndrome: Alyssa Siegel, "A New Understanding and Perhaps a Word for Down Syndrome in Ethiopia," Children's Hospital of Philadelphia, January 24, 2021, https://www.chop.edu /news/new-understanding-and-perhaps-word-down-syndrome-ethiopia.

60 cannot get surgery: "Suffer for Good," rickhodes.org, accessed February 11, 2025, https://rickhodes.org/suffer-for-good.

60 "hole in the heart": Global Down Syndrome Foundation, "Congenital Heart Defects and Down Syndrome: What Parents Should Know," *Down Syndrome World*, no. 3 (2018), https://www.globaldownsyndrome .org/congenital-heart-defects-syndrome-parents-know/.

62 "saves the world entire": "Dr. Rick Hodes: Saving Lives, One Person at a Time," Jewish Colorado, June 21, 2023, https://www.jewishcolorado .org/dr-rick-hodes-saving-lives-one-person-at-a-time/.

Chapter 6: Team 43

74 17.2 suicide deaths: "The Truth About Suicide and Guns," Brady United, n.d., accessed February 18, 2025, https://www.bradyunited.org /resources/research/the-truth-about-suicide-and-guns.

74 30,177 post-9/11 war veterans: Thomas Howard Suitt, III, "High Suicide Rates Among United States Service Members and Veterans of the Post-9/11 Wars," The Watson School of International and Public Affairs, June 21, 2021, https://watson.brown.edu/costsofwar/files/cow /imce/papers/2021/Suitt_Suicides_Costs%20of%20War_June%2021 %202021.pdf.

74 less likely to have sought treatment: Patrice Harley, "People Who Die by Suicide with a Firearm Are Less Likely to Have Sought Treatment," news release, Rutgers University, March 14, 2022, https://www.rutgers.edu/news/people-who-die-suicide-firearm-are-less-likely-have-sought-treatment.

74 majority of suicide attempts: Elizabeth Hlavinka, "9 out of 10 Suicide Attempts Using Firearms Are Lethal," MedPage Today, December 3, 2019, https://www.medpagetoday.com/psychiatry/generalpsychiatry/83665.

74 Eight out of ten: "Firearms, Accidental Deaths, Suicides and Violent Crime: An Updated Review of the Literature with Special Reference to the Canadian Situation," Department of Justice Canada, 1998, accessed February 18, 2025, https://www.justice.gc.ca/eng/rp-pr/csj-sjc/jsp-sjp/wd98_4-dt98_4/p4.html.

75 85 percent of users relapse: Rajita Sinha, "New Findings on Biological Factors Predicting Addiction Relapse Vulnerability," *Current Psychiatry Reports* 13, no. 5 (2011): 398–405, https://doi.org/10.1007/s11920-011-0224-0.

Chapter 9: Dodie Osteen and Her World of Healing

114 every 60,000 to 100,000 cases: Akira Sakamaki et al., "Spontaneous Regression of Hepatocellular Carcinoma: A Mini-Review," *World Journal of Gastroenterology* 23, no. 21 (2017): 3797–3804, https://www.ncbi.nlm.nih.gov/pmc/articles/PMC5467065/.

Chapter 11: Dr. Ellay Hogeg-Golan

139 deep partial-thickness: MediWound, "MediWound Announces NexoBrid Marketing Approval from Israeli Ministry of Health," press release, July 16, 2014, https://ir.mediwound.com/news-releases/news-release-details/mediwound-announces-nexobrid-marketing-approval-israeli-ministry.

146 "to care for these patients": Audra Clark et al., "Nutrition and Metabolism in Burn Patients," *Burns & Trauma* 5 (2017), https://doi.org/10.1186/s41038-017-0076-x.

Chapter 12: Montgomery MD

160 100,000 people on the national transplant list: "Organ Donation Statistics," OrganDonor.gov, Health Resources and Services Administration, accessed April 1, 2025. https://www.organdonor.gov/learn/organ-donation-statistics.

161 In 2022, Dr. Moazami and others: NYU Langone Health, "First-Ever Combined Heart Pump and Gene-Edited Pig Kidney Transplant Gives New Hope to Patient with Terminal Illness," press release, April

24, 2024, https://nyulangone.org/news/first-ever-combined-heart-pump-gene-edited-pig-kidney-transplant-gives-new-hope-patient-terminal-illness.

Chapter 13: Dan the Man

168 77 percent of American adults: Michael Prasad, "The Role of Faith in Disasters," Domestic Preparedness, November 9, 2022, https://domesticpreparedness.com/emergency-management/resilience-the-role-of-faith-in-disasters.

170 Multiple studies: Krishanu Chaudhuri et al., "Survival of Trauma Patients with Coma and Bilateral Fixed Dilated Pupils," *Injury* 40, no. 1 (2009): 28–32, doi:10.1016/j.injury.2008.09.004.

170 "Patients with head injury": Demetrios Demetriades et al., "Outcome and Prognostic Factors in Head Injuries with an Admission Glasgow Coma Scale Score of 3," *Archives of Surgery* 139, no. 10 (2004):1066–68, doi:10.1001/archsurg.139.10.1066.

170 40 percent survival rate: H. Clusmann et al., "Fixed and Dilated Pupils After Trauma, Stroke, and Previous Intracranial Surgery: Management and Outcome," *Journal of Neurology, Neurosurgery, and Psychiatry* 71, no. 2 (2001): 175–81, doi:10.1136/jnnp.71.2.175.

170 with the diuretic mannitol: C. Ong et al., "Effects of Osmotic Therapy on Pupil Reactivity: Quantification Using Pupillometry in Critically Ill Neurologic Patients," *Neurocritical Care* 30 (2019): 307–15, https://doi.org/10.1007/s12028-018-0620-y.

171 improve outcomes dramatically: P. J. Hutchinson et al., "Opening the Skull of Patients After Head Injury Reduces Risk of Death from Brain Swelling," University of Cambridge, September 8, 2016, https://www.cam.ac.uk/research/news/opening-the-skull-of-patients-after-head-injury-reduces-risk-of-death-from-brain-swelling.

Chapter 16: Back from the Dead

226 "The nature of this invention": Jan Bondeson, *Buried Alive: The Terrifying History of Our Most Primal Fear* (New York: Norton, 2001).

228 invented a model: Kate Cherrell, "Buried Alive! A Short History of Premature Burial and Safety Coffins," Burials and Beyond, March 27, 2019, https://burialsandbeyond.com/2019/03/27/buried-alive-a-short-history-of-premature-burial-and-safety-coffins/comment-page-1/.

ABOUT THE AUTHOR

DR. MARC SIEGEL is the senior medical analyst for Fox News and a clinical professor of medicine and practicing internist at NYU Langone Health, where he is the medical director of *Doctor Radio* on SiriusXM. He has interviewed top health experts and public officials, as well as spiritual healers and medical missionaries. Dr. Siegel has also interviewed President Donald Trump, former president George W. Bush, three Health and Human Services secretaries, and heads of the NIH, CDC, and FDA, all for Fox News. He is a member of the board of contributors at *USA Today*, a columnist for FoxNews.com, *The Hill*, and *The Wall Street Journal*. Dr. Siegel graduated from SUNY Buffalo School of Medicine and completed his residency training at the NYU Langone Medical Center, where he has been a member of the teaching and clinical faculty for more than thirty years.